KAZAKHSTAN

Guek-Cheng Pang

MARSHALL CAVENDISH
New York • London • Sydney

Reference edition published 2001 by
Marshall Cavendish Corporation
99 White Plains Road
Tarrytown
New York 10591

© Times Media Private Limited 2001

Originated and designed by
Times Books International, an imprint of
Times Media Private Limited, a member of the
Times Publishing Group

Printed in Malaysia

Library of Congress Cataloging-in-Publication Data:
Cheng, Pang Guek, 1950–
   Kazakhstan / Guek-Cheng Pang.
      p. cm. — (Cultures of the world)
   Includes bibliographical references and index.
   ISBN 0-7614-1193-3
   1. Kazakhstan—Juvenile literature. [1. Kazakhstan.] I. Title.
II. Series.

DK903.C49 2001
958.45—dc21

                              00-047458
                              CIP
                              AC

INTRODUCTION

FOR CENTURIES, HUNS, TURKS, AND MONGOLS fought among themselves and ignored the world. When the fighting subsided in the 15th century, a people who prided themselves on being different emerged. They called themselves Kazakhs—independent and free wanderers. By the second half of the 19th century, however, Kazakhstan became a colony of the Russian Empire. The Kazakhs were forced into a sedentary life that they abhorred and had to endure famines, watch as their lands were forcibly taken away and ruined, and their customs and traditions suppressed. Their country became the dumping ground of millions of people, so much so that they became a minority in their own land.

Fortunately, with the breakup of the Soviet Union in 1991, independence and liberation arrived. The challenge for Kazakhs today is to rediscover their culture and manage their vast land rich in natural resources.

CONTENTS

A Kazakh girl in winter wear. The average January temperature in Kazakhstan can go as low as -2°F (-19°).

CONTENTS

Kazakh elders are treated with much respect by the younger generation, and their advice is often sought and heeded.

GEOGRAPHY

KAZAKHSTAN IS A LARGE, LANDLOCKED COUNTRY in the middle of Central Asia. Its area is 1,048,878 square miles (2,717,300 square km), slightly less than four times the size of Texas.

From the Ural Mountains in the north to the bordering countries of Uzbekistan and Kyrgyzstan in the south, it measures 1,242 miles (2,000 km). From the border with China in the east to the shores of the Caspian Sea in the west, the distance is 1,863 miles (3,000 km) wide.

Kazakhstan used to be a part of the Soviet Union before its breakup in 1991. Today Kazakhstan's population of 16.8 million makes it the third most populous republic in the newly created Commonwealth of Independent States (CIS), which includes Armenia, Azerbaijan, Belarus, Georgia, Kyrgyzstan, Moldova, the Russian Federation, Tajikistan, Turkmenistan, the Ukraine, and Uzbekistan.

Left: **An unusual rock formation in Lake Borovoye.**

Opposite: **Kazakhstan is the largest state in Central Asia and the ninth largest country in the world.**

VARIED LANDSCAPES

About 44% of Kazakhstan is desert, while 9% of the country consists of mixed prairie and forest or treeless prairie. Mountainous regions form 12.4% of the landscape. The Tien Shan mountain chain, lying along the border of Kazakhstan, Kyrgyzstan, and China, rises mightily in the southeast. The Altai (or Altay) mountain system, with three distinctive ridges, is in the northeast. Also in the east is Lake Balkhash, a huge, shallow pool that is distinctive because the eastern half is salty, while the western half consists of fresh water. Farther inland are the Chingiz-Tau Mountains, rising to about 5,000 feet (1,523 m). The Caspian Depression, a dominant

Steppes account for about 26% of the total land area of Kazakhstan.

feature in the west and southwest, is as much as 95 feet (29 m) below sea level at its lowest point. South of the depression are the Ustyurt Plateau and Tupqaraghan Peninsula, which borders the Caspian Sea. The Greater Barsuki Desert and the Kyzylkum Desert are located near the Aral Sea, while the Muyunkum Desert and the Betpaqdala Desert lies in south-central Kazakhstan.

RICHES BENEATH THE LAND

In the north the landscape is a mixture of forests and steppe. This is the most fertile region in the country, although the soil system is very fragile. It is also the most heavily cultivated and agriculturally most productive region. As one travels south, the grasslands change to desert and semi-desert areas. Unsuitable for agriculture, the deserts are vast, empty, and desolate, and little has changed since the days when Genghis Khan and his Mongol hordes swept through Central Asia. But underneath this seeming wasteland lies huge reserves of oil, gas, and other rich mineral resources.

Many of the peaks in the Tien Shan and Altai ranges are snow-covered all year.

SNOW-COVERED MOUNTAINS

In the east and southeast, the rich lowlands give way to hills and foothills, eventually rising to the Tien Shan and Altai mountain ranges that Kazakhstan shares with its neighbors China and Russia. Kazakhstan's most beautiful scenery can be found in this region.

The Tien Shan Mountains, or "Heavenly Mountains" in Chinese, is the major mountain system in Central Asia. It stretches over 1,490 miles (2,400 km), through China, Kyrgyzstan, and Kazakhstan. The highest point in Kazakhstan, the 22,958-feet (6,995-m) Pik Khan-Tengri, is located in the Tien Shan range, but it is not the highest peak in these mountains. That is Peak Pobedy—Russian for victory—which rises to 24,415 feet (7,439 m) in eastern Kyrgyzstan. The Altai Mountains are a gentle range, with more woods and meadows than rocks and ravines.

DISAPPEARING LAKES

There are three major river systems. In the west the Ural and Emba rivers flow through the Caspian Depression before ending their journey in the Caspian Sea. In the southeast several rivers flow out of the highlands. Of these, the largest rivers are the Chu and the Syr Darya. The Chu ends in the Muyunkum Desert and the Betpaqdala Basin. The Syr Darya empties into the Aral Sea. The third system flows from the Tien Shan Mountains into Lake Balkhash. The Ili and Ayaguz rivers are the largest in this system.

Kazakhstan has 48,000 lakes, but most of these have an area of less than a square mile (2.6 square km). Those in the lowlands and the deserts are usually salty lakes, while those in the north and in the mountains are fed with fresh water from the snow. The Caspian and Aral seas and Lake Balkhash are the three largest bodies of water in the country.

For most of the year, the lakes are marshy bogs and may even evaporate completely in the summer.

Autumn in Kazakhstan. The land experiences extreme seasonal changes, with harsh winters and scorching summers.

CLIMATE

A landlocked country located at a great distance from the sea, Kazakhstan has a continental climate. This means it is affected by the large land masses surrounding it rather than oceans. It is very cold in the winter, especially in the north where temperatures can drop to -58°F (-50°C). In the summer, especially in the southern deserts, it can be as hot as 113°F (45°C).

Kazakhstan is also a dry country, especially in the south-central region, which receives only about 4 inches (10 cm) of rain annually. The country is so far inland that moisture-laden ocean winds drop their rainwater long before they reach Kazakhstan. The lack of rain means that most days are sunny and the skies are often blue and cloudless. The wettest part of the country is in the mountainous eastern region, which gets as much as 24 inches (61 cm) of precipitation a year, mainly in the form of snow.

FLORA AND FAUNA

Kazakhstan is rich in flora and fauna. Eight nature reserves have been established to try to protect the uniqueness of the land. There are more than 6,000 species of plants, of which 535 are found only in Kazakhstan. About 155 species of mammals, 480 species of birds, and 150 species of fish add to the diversity.

The country has few forests; it is mostly grassland, with dry shrubby wormwood, Russian thistle, black saxaul, and tamarisk growing on the plains and in the deserts and feather grass on the drier plains. Naurzum Nature Reserve in the Kustanay region was established in 1934 to protect the pine forests there. The area shelters several rare animals such as the mouflon, a kind of wild sheep, the long-needled hedgehog, and wildcats like the caracal and barkhan, or sand cat, and the beautiful bustard, a game bird.

THE GOLDEN EAGLE

The golden eagle is one of Kazakhstan's national symbols and appears on the national flag. Kazakhs revere the eagle as a symbol of power and strength because it is the master of the skies. The female bird is larger than the male, measuring 3 feet (1 m) from beak to tail. The eagle has a wingspan of 7 feet (2 m). Its overall color is dark brown, but the feathers over the back of the head and neck are a distinct golden color, hence its name. Golden eagles nest in the high, mountainous country on cliff ledges and in the tops of tall trees. They can also be found in the mountainous regions in northwest United States, Canada, and Mexico.

The reindeer is found in the highlands of Kazakhstan.

The Tien Shan Mountains are home to the endangered snow leopard, Tien Shan brown bear, Siberian stag, bearded vulture with a wing span of over 10 feet (3 m), Himalayan ular or mountain turkey-hen, and golden eagle, favorite bird of Kazakh hunters. In the Altai Mountains can be found the giant Siberian stag, also called an *elik*, and the small musk deer. Lake Alakol in the southeast is a nature reserve and is the habitat for rare birds such as the fish hawk and the black stork.

The fresh and saltwater lakes of the steppes attract all kinds of migrating birds. In addition, there are numerous species of ducks, geese, herons, gulls, sandpipers, and terns. Lake Tengiz in central Kazakhstan attracts millions of migratory birds every year and hosts the northernmost nesting colony of pink flamingos that make their nests here. Birds of prey circle the skies—eagles, merlins, kestrels, and others. Large herds of Saiga antelope and elk roam the plains.

The deserts are home to hordes of Middle Asian gazelle. There are also many species of jerboas, polecats, and birds such as the jay, lark, and desert dove. One of the world's largest lizards, the grey monitor lizard, lives in the Kyzylkum Desert. There are many other species of lizards and snakes.

Fishermen catch sturgeon, trout, carp, herring, and roach in the seas, rivers and lakes. The sheatfish, a type of catfish that can grow to more than 6.6 feet (2 m) long and weigh more than 440 pounds (200 kg), is a game fish sought by anglers fishing in the Ili river system.

MAJOR CITIES AND TOWNS

Before the 20th century, Kazakhstan had few large cities. The Kazakhs were nomads and lived in *yurts*, which are tent-like structures, or in small villages that centered on farming or that were located on trade routes. After World War II, an influx of Russian industrial workers resulted in a rapid growth of cities. Now, more than half the population lives in cities.

The towns are small settlements or villages separated by large areas of cultivated land in the north or inhospitable plains and deserts in the south. Typical Soviet-planned towns, such as Karanganda and Oskemen, have straight, wide streets that are bordered by nondescript gray buildings several stories high and surrounded by industrial zones.

A modern village in northern Kazakhstan.

Astana has a long history, as it was located along the old Steppe Route that was in use long before the famous Silk Road.

ASTANA The town of Akmola was renamed Astana (which means "capital" in Kazakh) and made the capital of the country in May 1998 by a decree of the president of the republic, Nursultan Nazarbayev.

Astana has undergone several name changes. It was known as Akmolinsk before becoming Tselinograd in 1961, and then Akmola in 1992. It is at the junction of the Trans-Kazakhstan and South Siberian railroads, along the banks of the Ishim (Esil) River in the north-central part of the country. The town was originally a Russian military outpost in the 19th century and later became an administrative center for the region. It became particularly important in the 1950s when the Soviet Union adopted a Virgin Lands policy. There was a tremendous amount of building activity and several research and educational institutions were established in the city. Today there are metal-finishing factories there that process copper, gold, and bauxite from mines in the region. Most of the townspeople work on the railroad and in factories. The population of Astana was 271,000 in 1997.

ALMATY, the former capital of Kazakhstan, has 1.13 million inhabitants. It was named Almaty after the apple trees for which it is famous. In 1854 the Russians established a frontier post in Almaty and called it Vernyi. Soon after a fort was established, Cossacks and Siberian peasant farmers settled in the area. The town was devastated by two earthquakes in 1887 and 1911. In 1921, when the Soviets occupied the town, they changed the name to Alma-ata, meaning "father of apples." In 1929 Alma-ata became the capital of Soviet Kazakhstan. In 1992 the town regained its name of Almaty.

The city is an orderly grid pattern of roads that slope from south to north. Its citizens are mostly industrial workers who work in the tobacco, lumber, and heavy machinery manufacturing industries. Since independence Almaty has developed an air of cosmopolitanism and a spirit of adventure. Many visitors come here in search of opportunities—Chinese Uighur traders from Urumchi, in Xinjiang, sell their wares in the bazaar; foreign experts are eager to advise the government; and Western businesspeople hope to clinch some business deals.

An aerial view of Almaty, the country's cultural center. It houses many museums and theaters.

The air pollution in Dzambul is causing frighteningly high levels of cancer and lung disease.

SHYMKENT The city of Shymkent (formerly Chimkent) in the south lies along the route of the TurkSib railroad. It was founded in the 12th century on the strength of trade between the nomads and the citizens of Kokand in Uzbekistan. But this once pretty little town was completely destroyed by heavy Russian shelling in 1864. It has been rebuilt since World War II. Today the main industry is lead smelting from ore mined in the nearby Karatau Hills. The lead is used to make bullets. Shymkent's 322,000 citizens wake up on most days to a pall of grey-brown fumes that hang in the air, a result of pollution caused by the lead smelting industry in the south of the city. There are also chemical works and fruit canneries.

DZHAMBUL,or Zhambyl, is an old city built in the sixth century when it was known as Taraz. It claims to have been a capital of the Turks in the 11th century, but this distinction is also claimed by the cities of Bukhara in Uzbekistan and Balasagun in Kyrgyzstan. Dzhambul was practically destroyed by the Mongols in the 13th century and renamed Aulie-Ata in 1864 by the Russians. When Kazakhstan became a republic in 1936, it was renamed Dzhambul after a local folk singer, Dzhababayev Dzhambul. The town has also undergone changes in appearance, from a majestic city of mosques and minarets to one filled with apartment blocks where industry pollutes the air. Three chemical factories produce fertilizer from phosphate ore found in the nearby mountains and dirty the air for the 307,000 people in the city. Dzhambul and Fresno in California are sister cities.

SEMEY, 621 miles (1,000 km) north of Almaty and littered with log houses, is probably the most Russian-looking of Kazakh towns. It was founded as a Russian fort in 1718 during the reign of Peter the Great and was originally called Semipalatinsk (*palatka* means tent) because of the tents that were erected around the fort. It became an important trading town in the late

19th century. Its most famous inhabitant was Fyodor Dostoyevsky, a Russian author who was exiled to this place in 1854. Dostoyevsky lived in Semipalatinsk from 1857 to 1859 in a wooden house. Today there is a museum, the F. M. Dostoyevsky Memorial Museum, that includes the house in which he lived. It tells of his life and the time he spent in Semipalatinsk. In more recent years, the town was infamous for the secret nuclear testing done nearby in 1949. Fortunately, this controversy ended in 1990, but not before statistics showed a higher than average incidence of cancer among its people. Semey, with a population of 334,000, has food-processing, leather, textile, and lumber factories.

A street vendor in Semey.

HISTORY

THERE HAVE BEEN RECORDS of human habitation in Kazakhstan since the Stone Age. Petroglyphs, stone monuments, and other cultural artifacts testify to the existence of a nomadic people who tended animals and moved with the seasons because this was the most suitable lifestyle for them.

In the fifth century A.D. the Huns, a nomadic Asian people, under their fierce warrior leader Attila, attacked the great Roman Empire. The Huns were succeeded by tribes of Turkic-speaking people who were organized into political units known as khanates. In the centuries that followed, several regions of Kazakhstan belonged to different empires. During the 15th century, most of it was part of the Mongol Empire. The Kazakhs, who were in fact Uzbeks who were dissatisfied with their khan, or ruler, did not arrive in Kazakhstan until the 15th century.

Left: **Pope Leo I dissuading Attila the Hun from attacking the Roman Empire.**

Opposite: **A monument in Republic Square, commemorating the heroes who died in the past wars in Kazakhstan.**

GENGHIS KHAN AND THE SILK ROAD

The earliest state that historians are aware of in the region was that of the Turkic Khanate, established in the sixth century A.D. In the eighth century the Kazakhstan region attracted the attention of the outside world because it lay along the Silk Road that connected Europe to China. This route passed near Almaty.

For the next few centuries, various parts of the region were dominated by confederations of Turkic tribes and Arabs who introduced Islam to the region. They fought among themselves until Mongol armies invaded the area under the banner of Genghis Khan in the 13th century and imposed Mongol customs and language on the people.

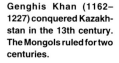

Genghis Khan (1162–1227) conquered Kazakhstan in the 13th century. The Mongols ruled for two centuries.

After the Mongol invasion, the tribes in the area came under the control of a succession of khans of the western branch of the Mongol Empire, called the Golden Horde. The Golden Horde later split into smaller groups, including the Nogai Horde and the Uzbek Khanate.

KAZAKHS BREAK AWAY

The Kazakhs emerged as a recognizable group in the mid-15th century when some of the tribes broke away from the khanates and sought independence.

The breakaway was led by Janibek and Ghireis, two sons of the Barak Khan of the White Horde of the Mongol Empire. They led their people in a revolt against Abul Khayr of the Uzbek Khanate. Kazakhs believe this to be the beginning of the their nation.

A Mongol camp on the move.

Janibek and Ghirei led their supporters to the land near the Chu River. As time went on, their supporters and the territory they controlled grew. Although they belonged to the Uzbek tribe, they were also called Kazakhs because the word meant a people who had wandered away and who were free and independent. The Kazakhs had a more nomadic lifestyle than the Uzbeks, who were more sedentary.

Their first leader was Khan Kasym, who united the Kazakh tribes. During the late 15th century and throughout the 16th century, the Kazakhs were a strong, nomadic empire that ruled the steppes from the shores of the Caspian and Aral seas in the south and west to the upper Ertis River in the east. Khan Kasym was believed to have in his service more than 200,000 warrior horsemen who were feared by all their neighbors.

Russians in traditional costume.

THREE HORDES EMERGE

This unity, however, was shortlived. During the successive reigns of Khan Kasym's three sons, the Kazakhs soon separated into three new tribal federations called the Great Horde, which controlled the southeastern region north of the Tien Shan Mountains; the Middle Horde, which ruled in the north-central region east of the Aral Sea; and the Lesser Horde, which occupied the west between the Aral Sea and the Ural River.

This was the situation until the 17th century when Russian traders and soldiers appeared on the scene. The Russians set up an outpost on the north coast of the Caspian Sea in 1645 and from then on built more forts and seized control of more and more Kazakh territory. In the late 16th and 17th century, the Kazakhs were in conflict with Kalmyk invaders of Mongol origin.

From the 1680s to the 1770s the Kazakhs were at war with the Oyrat federation of four western Mongol tribes. The Russians gained increasing control because the Kazakhs were pressured from the east by the Mongols, forcing them westwards. In 1730 Abul Khayr of the Lesser Horde sought Russian help. This alliance unfortunately gave the Russians permanent control over the Lesser Horde. In 1732 part of the Middle Horde was incorporated by Russia, while another part was incorporated by the oath of the Sultan and elders. The Russians conquered the Middle Horde by 1798. The Great Horde managed to remain independent until the 1820s, when the expanding Qugen (Kokend) Khanate in the south forced them to choose Russian protection.

RUSSIANS ESTABLISH A FOOTHOLD

Life on the steppes continued without too much interference from the Russians until the 1820s, when the Russians decided to introduce a new system of administration. The land was divided into administrative units that allowed the Czarist government to tax the people, and Russian military rule was imposed. The three khanates were abolished: the Middle Horde in 1822; the Lesser Horde in 1824; and the Great Horde in 1848.

The Kazakhs resisted Russian rule from the beginning. The first big revolt was led by Khan Kene of the Middle Horde between the years 1837 and 1847. Despite Kazakh resistance, the Russians continued to colonize the land and built a series of forts. Khan Kene was killed in 1847 after a bitter struggle and became the first Kazakh hero.

The construction of Russian forts began the destruction of the nomadic life of the people by limiting the area over which the tribes could graze their animals. When Russians settled the fertile lands of northern and eastern Kazakhstan in the 1890s, it signaled the complete destruction of nomadic life there. Then, between 1906 and 1912, more than half a million farms were established by the Russians. As increasing numbers of Russian and Ukrainian peasants arrived, the Kazakhs were compelled to emigrate east to China.

When the Russian government tried to recruit the Kazakhs in 1916 to fight against Germany, the people, already starving and displaced from their lands, resisted conscription into the Russian Imperial Army. This resistance, led by Amangeldy Imanov, was brutally crushed. Thousands of Kazakhs were killed, while thousands of others fled to China and Mongolia. As a punishment, those nomads who had taken part in the revolt were driven from their lands and the area was made available to Russian settlers.

Khan Kene was also known as Kenisary Kasimov.

In 1917, when news of the Russian Revolution and the collapse of Imperial Russia reached Kazakhstan, the Kazakhs, led by their Westernized intelligentsia, revolted. Under the leadership of Ali Khan Bukeikhanov, they set up a party called Alash Orda (Horde of Alash).

The Bolsheviks took over power in Russia in October 1917 and began to set up revolutionary committees and armed units in Kazakhstan. They allowed the Kazakhs to establish an independent state, called Alash Orda. The Alash Orda survived for two years, from 1918–20, before it was suppressed by the Soviets. The Kazakhs accepted Soviet rule, and some of its leaders became communists.

The years of fighting took its toll on the Kazakhs, who suffered heavy material losses as well as loss of their loved ones. Although they did not take part in the Russian Revolution, many Kazakhs died in the famine that followed the civil war.

Despite their nomadic lifestyle, most Kazakhs are literate.

THE SOVIET ERA

In 1936 Kazakhstan became a Soviet republic. During this period, the leaders of the republic were mostly foreigners rather than Kazakhs.

From 1929 to 1937 Russian agriculture was collectivized under a policy launched by Soviet leader Joseph Stalin. The Kazakhs suffered because the peasants killed their livestock to protest this policy, and thousands fled to China and Afghanistan. It is estimated that at least 1.5 million Kazakhs and 80% of the country's livestock died during this period.

The Soviets also discouraged nomadic life and encouraged permanent settlement. They pursued an antireligious policy, arresting religious leaders and anyone suspected of being a nationalist. All religious organizations were closed to force people to conform.

To develop the economy, the government promoted industrialization. As industry expanded, skilled workers immigrated to the country. During World War II, much of Russia's industry was moved to Kazakhstan to prevent its capture by the Germans.

Above: **Leonid Brezhnev died in 1982, when he was still head of the Communist Party.**

Opposite: **Mikhail Gorbachev was president of the Soviet Union from 1985–91.**

FORCED EMIGRATION

Various other peoples—Crimean Tatars, Volga Germans, Poles, Ukrainians, Koreans, and Muslims—were resettled in the Kazakh region because the Russians distrusted them or were afraid that they would collaborate with Germany during World War II. Other Muslims from neighboring countries, including those from Azerbaijan, and Uighurs from China also immigrated to Kazakhstan.

Between 1953 and 1965 the Soviet campaign to increase the production of wheat and other grains led to large areas of grazing land in the vast grasslands in northern Kazakhstan being put under the plow. This was the Virgin and Idle Lands program. In 1954 Nikita Khrushchev, who was then First Secretary of the Communist Party, sent his assistant Leonid Brezhnev as his representative to Kazakh SSR (Soviet Socialist Republic) to supervise the Virgin and Idle Lands experiment. This program brought another influx of Russian and Ukrainian farmers to the region. After Brezhnev was recalled to Moscow, a Kazakh named Dinmukhamed Kunayev became First Secretary of the Communist Party. However, as a result of the failure of the agricultural policies and other economic problems, Kunayev was forced to resign. He came back into power in 1964 and became the first Kazakh to become a full member of the ruling Politburo (parliament) of the Soviet Union. As a leader of great foresight and achievement, Kunayev looked after the needs of Kazakhs and Russians with equal care.

FAILED ECONOMY

Kunayev initially raised the standard of living of his people and instituted reforms in higher education that allowed more people to attend university and get better jobs. He stayed in power for over 20 years before coming under attack for mismanagement, favoritism, and misconduct when the economy failed under his leadership. In 1985 Gorbachev forced him to resign. His dismissal caused unrest—many people took to the streets to demonstrate, producing one of the most serious riots in the Soviet Union in the 1980s.

Kunayev was replaced with an ethnic Russian, Gennadiy Kolbin. Many people were against Kolbin's appointment and rioted and held demonstrations. There are conflicting reports as to how many people were killed, injured and arrested in this unrest. Some reports say at least 200 people died and more than 1,000 were injured. Kolbin was an administrator who instituted economic and social reforms that were Soviet-inspired and unrealistic, causing the economy to deteriorate further. Agricultural output continued to drop, so that in 1989 Kolbin suggested killing wild ducks that were migrating through the country to provide meat for people.

RISE OF NATIONALISM

Starting in 1989 conflicts developed in the Soviet Union between the central parliament of the USSR and the parliaments of the individual republics, mainly over the respective powers that each should have. There were increasing demands in the republics for autonomy and even for full independence. At the Congress of People's Deputies in Moscow in June 1989, many informal political groups presented their nationalist programs. This feeling of nationalism was also echoed in Kazakhstan.

In June 1989 Kolbin returned to Moscow and was replaced by Nursultan Nazarbayev. In March 1990 elections were held. A new legislature consisting of a majority of ethnic Kazakhs and a minority of Russians was formed.

NAZARBAYEV IN POWER

Nazarbayev, a Kazakh, trained as a metallurgist and an engineer, proved himself to be a skilled politician. He became a member of the Communist Party in 1979 and was made chairman of Kazakhstan's Council of Ministers in 1984. When Kunayev fell out of favor, Nazarbayev took a major role in the attacks against Kunayev. Although he was passed over in favor of Kolbin in 1986, Nazarbayev was a strong supporter of Gorbachev and his reform programs. He realized the importance of balancing Moscow's demands with increasing Kazakh nationalism. After he took over, he made Kazakh the official language, allowed for greater religious tolerance, and permitted criticism and an examination of the negative effects that collectivization and other Soviet policies had on the country.

The late 1980s was a time of tremendous turmoil in the Soviet Union, which was facing imminent breakup. Gorbachev attempted to hold the union together by calling for the election of a national legislature and a loosening of Soviet political control over the republics.

Throughout it all, Nazarbayev supported Gorbachev and the Soviet Union because he believed that the member republics were too economically dependent on each other to be able to survive on their own. But he was also aware of the importance of gaining control of the country's mineral wealth. In June 1991, at his insistence, Moscow surrendered control of the mineral resources in Kazakhstan.

In September 1991 the three republics of Estonia, Latvia, and Lithuania achieved complete independence and were recognized as sovereign states. Several other republics were demanding independence. Gorbachev tried to establish a new "union of sovereign states" that would have some common foreign, defense, and economic policies, but no agreement could be reached with the remaining republics.

On December 16, 1991, Kazakhstan declared independence. On December 21, 1991, 11 of the 15 republics, including Kazakhstan, signed documents for the dissolution of the Soviet Union and the establishment of the Commonwealth of Independent States (CIS) that would share a common policy for foreign affairs and defense.

GOVERNMENT

FOR MORE THAN TWO CENTURIES, Kazakhstan was under Russian control, first imperial Czarist rule, then communist Soviet rule. When independence was declared on December 16, 1991, Nursultan Nazarbayev became the country's first president, and Kazakhstan retained the basic govern-ment structure and most of the leaders who were in power under the Soviets.

CONSTITUTIONS OF 1993 AND 1995

The post-independence government of Kazakhstan consists of the president, who is the head of government; an executive branch, represented by the Council of Ministers; a legislative branch that is the parliament; and the judicial branch.

Left: **A patriotic poster with the national flags of Kazakhstan.**

Opposite: **President Nursultan Nazarbayev listens to the national anthem as he stands during an inauguration ceremony on January 20, 1999.**

President Nazarbayev giving an address during the opening ceremony of a building. The president has the authority to issue decrees and overrule actions taken by the ministries.

Two new constitutions, written in 1993 and 1995, have ensured the power of the president and his control over the government.

The 1993 constitution replaced the Soviet constitution, in force since 1978. Under this constitution, the prime minister and the Council of Ministers are responsible only to the president. A new constitution in 1995 reinforced this relationship and placed the country under direct presidential rule. The constitution was drawn up by President Nazarbayev and his Council of Ministers. It was adopted by popular referendum in August 1995. This constitution also guarantees equal rights to people of all nationalities and made Kazakh and Russian the official state languages.

Under the constitution, the president is the head of state. He is elected for a maximum of two consecutive, five-year terms. He governs with the help of the Council of Ministers, whose key members he appoints. The head of the council is the prime minister. The president appoints the prime minister and the other ministers of the council, as well as the chairperson of the National Security Committee.

TWO HOUSES OF PARLIAMENT

Parliament, as established by the 1995 constitution, is made up of two houses, the Senate and the Assembly or Majlis. There used to be 47 seats in the Senate, but after the provinces were reduced to 14 in 1997, the number of senators decreased to 37. They are chosen by joint sessions of the province's legislative bodies. Two senators are elected in each province. The 67 members of the Majlis are selected by popular election. Members of both houses serve four-year terms.

A person wishing to run for the Senate must be a citizen for at least five years, 30 years or older, have higher education, and have lived in the territory he or she wishes to represent for not less than three years. A member of the Majlis must be a citizen and at least 25 years old. All Kazakh citizens 18 years and above are eligible to vote.

Members of the Senate and Majlis deal with the making of laws and their reform, the economy and the budget, international affairs, defense and security, regional development, and local administration.

ACTIVE POLITICAL CLIMATE

While the president has not encouraged a democratic society, he has balanced his authoritarian rule with allowance for opposition. However, opposition parties are not major players in the Kazakhstan Parliament.

The political change that Kazakhstan has undergone since independence has led to a proliferation of social organizations, political parties, and special interest groups. There are about 20 active political parties that have formed, reformed, split, and combined. Some special interest groups include the Russian Cossacks, Pensioners Movement, and Peasant Union. Political groups are the Legal Development of Kazakhstan, the Independent Miners Union, and several human rights groups.

Kazakh teenagers hold a portrait of President Nazarbayev and posters saying, "We are for Nazarbayev" during a show organized to support his 1999 election campaign.

THE JUDICIAL BRANCH

Before 1995 there were three high courts in Kazakhstan—the Supreme Court, the State Arbitrage Court, and the Constitutional Court. Together they employed 66 senior judges.

The 1995 constitution eliminated the State Arbitrage Court, which used to hear cases involving economic disputes between companies and the government and disputes between companies. The constitution retains the practice of presidential appointment of all judges in the republic and does not give term limits, suggesting that judges serve at the President's pleasure. Small local courts hear cases of petty crime, such as vandalism, while provincial courts deal with bigger crimes, like murders. Cases of appeal are sent to the Supreme Court. The judicial branch also includes the Constitutional Council.

The Ministry of Justice building.

A woman protesting against wrongful dismissal by going on a hunger strike. Such cases are usually handled by special human rights committees.

CONSTITUTIONAL COUNCIL

The Constitutional Council consists of seven judges. Two are nominated by the president, two by the chairman of the Senate, and two by the chairman of the Majlis. The chairman of the council is appointed by the president and is very powerful because he has the deciding vote if the council members are deadlocked over a case. The council members serve for six years. Half the members are appointed every three years. The 1995 constitution makes all former presidents of the republic automatic members of the council for life.

Council members may not be members of parliament, nor can they hold other employment except for some teaching, scientific, or creative activity. They may not be engaged in any private business or sit on an advisory council of a commercial enterprise.

It is the responsibility of the Constitutional Council to settle disputes about presidential and general elections, as well as those among parliamentary deputies. Besides ensuring that the laws to be adopted conform to the constitution, the council has to interpret the constitution and resolve all matters regarding constitutional procedures.

Besides the Constitutional Council, there are a number of advisory bodies under the direct control of the president. These are the Security Council, concerned with matters of defense and national security; the High Court Council; the National Council for State (National) Policy; and special committees dealing with mass media, and issues of human rights, family, and women.

LOCAL ADMINISTRATION

The country is divided into 14 provinces. The cities of Almaty and Leninsk have a special administrative status that is equal to a province. Each province is subdivided into regions and smaller administrative units of settlements. Every province has its own council responsible for budget, tax, and other administrative matters.

The heads of local administration, known as *hakim* ("ha-KEEM"), are appointed by the president and can only be removed from office by a two-thirds majority vote of no confidence by the local councils.

Kazakh children.

SMALL ARMY

Kazakh cadets shout as they parade before officers during their graduation ceremony. Some Kazakh cadets will receive further training in Turkey and Germany.

When Kazakhstan became independent in 1991, it had no military force because its defense and security matters had been taken care of by the Soviet army. A Kazakh military force was established in 1992 when the former Soviet 40th Army, stationed on Kazakh soil, was nationalized. Kazakhstan now has a general-purpose army, border troops, a small air force, and a navy for patrolling the Caspian Sea. But it continues to be dependent on Russia. In 1995 the two countries signed an agreement, and Russian troops now join Kazakhs in patrolling the country's borders.

RELATIONS WITH NEIGHBORS

Despite the breakup of the Soviet Union, Kazakhstan's ties with the former members of the union are still strong, and there are bilateral trade and security agreements with these countries. In 1994 Kazakhstan, Uzbekistan, and Kyrgyzstan set up a free-trade zone. Kazakhstan also tries to play a part in maintaining peace in the region. With Russia and Uzbekistan, it has tried to mediate in the civil war in Tajikistan.

Kazakhstan's relationship with China has been a careful one. The Chinese are next door neighbors, and Kazakhstan has always been wary of the possibility of Chinese domination. There are many Kazakhs living across the border in China, and since independence many Chinese have bought property in Kazakhstan and are living there. There is also a lot of trade between the two countries, as well as direct road and rail links.

Kakakhstan has received financial aid from Iran in developing transportation links, Oman in building oil pipeline, Egypt in building mosques, and Saudi Arabia in developing a national banking system.

Russian Defense Minister Igor Sergeyev shares a joke with his Chinese counterpart Chi Haotian. The defense ministers were in Astana for a meeting between the member states of the Shanghai Five group, consisting of China, Russia, Kazakhstan, Kyrgyzstan, and Tajikistan.

ECONOMY

KAZAKHSTAN HAS ENORMOUS RESERVES of fossil fuel, minerals, coal, and metals—iron ore, manganese, nickel, cobalt, copper, molybdenum, lead, zinc, bauxite, gold, uranium, phosphate, and silver.

For most of its modern history, Kazakhstan's economy was closely tied to that of the Soviet Union. Its resources were tapped and sent north to meet the production needs of Russian industry, which was developed to fulfil the demands of the Soviet consumer. Independence meant that Kazakhstan had to completely take charge of its economy and revamp its entire economic infrastructure.

RICH RESERVES

Of all its natural resources, oil is at present the country's most productive and lucrative. The oil reserves, found mainly in the northern end of the

Left: **The currency notes of Kazakhstan—the tenge.**

Opposite: **An oil refinery in Pavlodar, northeastern Kazakhstan.**

NEW "SILK ROAD"

The race is on to see who can benefit from the rich oil deposits in the Caspian Sea area. Kazakhstan and its neighbors, Azerbaijan and Turkmenistan, have enormous energy resources that until the breakup of the Soviet Union were exported from the region through Russian pipelines. Pipeline connections between the Tengiz oilfield and the Russian port of Novorossiysk are being improved by a group of international companies. China has signed an oil deal with Kazakhstan to construct a pipeline from Kazakhstan to the west of China. Other possible routes include moving the oil through Iran and Afghanistan. As US Energy Secretary Federico Pena said in November 1997 at a Caspian Pipeline conference: "We are building a new Silk Road, but the commodities now are not silk and spices, they are oil and gas. The paths will be taken not by camels and caravans, but by pipelines, fiber optics, and railroads."

Caspian Sea, have been estimated to be as much as 2.1 billion tons. Most of this is in new fields that have not yet been exploited.

Unfortunately, Kazakhhstan's oil and gas industry has traditionally depended on Russian demand for crude oil. Since the breakup of the Soviet Union, there has been a drop in production at Russian refineries. This has affected production levels in Kazakhstan although most of its oil is still exported to Russia.

Another problem for Kazakhstan in expanding the export of oil is that to reach Western customers, it has to rely on pipeline access through Russia. In the mid-1990s the only way to export oil was through the pipeline that connected Kazakh oil fields with the Russian Black Sea port of Novorossiysk.

Despite its enormous fuel reserves, Kazakhstan has to import oil and gas, because an undeveloped transportation network between the eastern and western parts of the country makes it difficult to use its own resources for industrial development. Kazakhstan has no pipelines to transport oil from the resource-rich west to the populated east.

Oil, natural gas, and other fuels are imported from Russia. Oil from the western oil fields is sent across the border to refineries in Russia, while Russian oil from Siberia feeds the refineries in eastern Kazakhstan.

Kazakhstan has enormous reserves of natural gas, especially in the northwest near the Russian border. The country also has three major coal fields in Torghay, Karaganda, and Ekibastuz. Much of the coal is used in

thermoelectric stations to produce power and to produce steel. Kazakhstan exports coal to Russia and to the other CIS states.

An open pit magnesium mine.

Phosphate, iron ore, manganese, chromite, lead, zinc, copper, titanium, bauxite, silver, phosphates, and cobalt are mined. Since independence, other foreign countries have shown interest in developing these resources with the Kazakh government.

INDUSTRY

Before 1991 Kazakhstan had a large manufacturing and processing industry. Following independence, industrial production remained the most important sector of the economy. There is a machine-building industry specializing in manufacturing construction equipment, tractors, bulldozers, agricultural machines, and military defense equipment. Metallurgy, or the processing of metals, and the production of chemicals, petrochemicals, and construction materials are also important. Light industries include the canning of fruit and vegetables, milling, brewing, and wine-making.

AGRICULTURE

Agriculture is the second most important segment of the economy after industry. The main agricultural regions are the north-central and southern parts of the country. Growing grain, especially wheat, is the main activity in the north-central region, while cotton and rice are the main crops in the south. Kazakhstan also produces meat, wool, and milk. Much of the agricultural land is under the control of the government. Farms are usually jointly owned state and collective farms or belong to farming associations.

The climate and soil is most suited to the grazing of animals, thus the traditional Kazakh nomadic lifestyle, where people follow their herds of sheep, cattle, camels, and horses as they graze on the open steppes. Nomadic life was disrupted when Soviet policy in the 1950s and 1960s introduced widespread cultivation of the land.

Growing cotton, one of the major crops in Kazakhstan. The vast country has enormous agricultural potential with its rich, steppe lands.

WORKFORCE

Most workers are employed in state enterprises, and before independence, women made up about half of the total number of workers. This high participation of women workers meant that about 80% of the population of working age were employed. But these high employment figures may not be accurate because until independence, it was Soviet policy not to acknowledge unemployment. Even now, there are employed people whose salaries have been reduced or stopped altogether or they may be on unpaid leave due to cutbacks in production.

In the past Russians tended to have higher-paying, skilled jobs in sectors such as transportation, industry, and science, while Kazakhs predominated in the lower-paid jobs. Since independence, large numbers of skilled managers and technicians, mainly of Russian or Slav descent, have moved out of the country, and this has affected the growth of the economy. But Kazakhs are quickly learning to fill in the gaps.

The labor force of Kazakhstan is almost 7 million, mostly employed in industry and manufacturing and in agriculture and forestry. The remaining workforce can be found in the construction, transportation, communications, trade, and service industries.

Cranes at the cargo port of Pavlodar. Kazakhstan exports mostly raw materials—ferrous and nonferrous metals, oil and petroleum products, and chemicals—and imports mostly manufactured goods—machinery, food, equipment vehicles, and chemicals.

BANKING

The National Bank of Kazakhstan regulates the country's banking system. The national banking system includes the State Export and Import Bank, the State Bank for Development, and small commercial banks.

The period immediately following independence was a time of great stress for the economy. Government price controls were removed, and a new, independent currency, the tenge, was introduced in 1993. The rate of inflation rose, and the price of food, services, and other products got so high that the people's buying power was greatly reduced.

TRADE

Russia continues to be Kazakhstan's biggest import and export partner. Other major CIS trading partners are Kyrgyzstan, Uzbekistan, Belarus, and the Ukraine, all of which import more from Kazakhstan than they export to it. Other important trading partners are China, Italy, Germany, Switzerland, the Czech Republic, and the Netherlands.

FOREIGN INVESTMENT

The country's stable government and the abundant natural resources have made Kazakhstan an attractive place for foreign investment. Companies from Great Britain, the United States, and France have all registered their interest in investing in the country. In 1994 Kazakhstan received a loan of more than US$1.33 billion from the Paris Club of Western creditor countries. This money is used in the reconstruction of the country's industrial and agricultural sectors.

BAYKONUR COSMODROME

Sending satellites into space is one of the more unusual ways Kazakhstan earns foreign exchange. It can put a satellite into orbit for any country and at a lower cost than that charged by the US National Aeronautics and Space Administration (NASA). Although the space facility is called Baykonur Cosmodrome, it is closer to the town of Leninsk; the town of Baykonur is 186 miles (299 km) north. The launch site used to be guarded with secrecy, but it has been open to the public since 1991 under certain conditions. The complex is a bewildering net-work of launch pads, gantries, and tracking stations. Launches literally shake the earth. The cosmodrome is funded and managed by the Russians.

POOR LINKS

The country's transportation and telecommunications networks are poorly developed. This is due to the generally inhospitable land that lies between populated areas. Only the largest cities are linked by both road and rail. Communication lines tend to run north to south, as Kazakhstan has traditionally looked north to Russia. Most freight is carried by rail, while people travel by road.

Before 1991 the only air route into Kazakhstan was via Moscow. In 1993 Kazakhstan Airlines was set up with 100 aircraft, part of the USSR's fleet that was divided among the former Soviet republics. Several private airline companies also operate in Kazakhstan, including the airlines of the Ukraine and Uzbekistan, Lufthansa of Germany, and Turkish Airlines.

It is also possible to travel by train from Russia and China. The Kazakh (formerly Turkistan-Siberian) railway, built with forced labor in the 1930s,

The international airlines serving Kazakhstan Airport fly between Almaty and several cities in Europe, including London and Frankfurt, as well as to Asia, China, Moscow, Turkey, Pakistan, and the other CIS states.

links Kazakhstan with the Trans-Siberian railway. The Urumchi-Almaty line was completed in 1990, linking Kazakhstan with Xinjiang in China via a border crossing at Druzhba (the name is Russian for "friendship"). There is also a border crossing by road to Xinjiang at Khorgos, 25 miles (40 km) from the Kazakh town of Panfilov.

Although Kazakhstan is landlocked, it has two inland river waterways—the Syr Darya River in the south-central region and the Ertis River in the north. They are used to transport freight and passengers.

Kazakhstan's telecommunications facilities are inadequate and old. In 1994 only 17 out of 100 people in the cities and fewer than eight out of every 100 in the rural areas had telephones. Telephone lines break down frequently, and spare parts are hard to get because much of the equipment is from the Soviet Union and Eastern Europe and is obsolete.

In 1994 there were almost 5 million television sets and twice as many radios. Kazakhstan is, however, well connected on the Internet. There are a number of Internet servers, and many websites, commercial and state-owned, offer a wealth of information about the country.

In Almaty buses and trolleys are the main forms of public transportation. Commercial buses will pick up passengers and allow them to alight anywhere along their route for a higher fare.

KAZAKHS

THERE ARE ABOUT 16,733,227 people living in Kazakhstan, but it is only since independence that indigenous Kazakhs have become the majority in their own country. When Kazakhstan was part of the Soviet Union, Russians, Ukrainians, and Belorussians formed more than half the population. Since 1991, many of them have returned to their homeland. At the same time, many Kazakhs from other parts of the world have returned to Kazakhstan.

Traditionally, Kazakh men wear a *chapan*, a wraparound robe made of cotton or wool and fastened with a belt at the waist. It looks like a dressing gown. The women wear colorful, sleeveless velvet jackets that are often ornately embroidered. The men wear caps on their heads and the women head scarves. Today it is usual to see Kazakhs in modern dress, and traditional clothing is not common.

Left and opposite: **Children under the age of 15 form 28% of the total population.**

HORDES

Historically, Kazakhs can be divided into three clans, or hordes. Each clan has its own territory. Kazakhs of the Lesser Horde come from western Kazakhstan, between the Aral Sea and the Ural River; the Middle Horde dominate the northern and central part of Kazakhstan east of the Aral Sea; the Great Horde belong to the southeastern area north of the Tien Shan Mountains.

Kazakhs of the Lesser and Middle Hordes were the first to come under Russian domination and tend to be more Russified. Many of their children were sent to study in Russian schools. Early Kazakh nationalists were often from these Lesser and Middle Hordes. They involved themselves in politics even before the Russian Revolution and were the targets of Stalin's purges during the 1930s when he tried to get rid of the Kazakh intelligentsia.

The Great Horde Kazakhs were the last to come under Russian control because, being in the south, they were farthest from Russia. They were politicized only after the revolution and were socialists. But members of the Great Horde have dominated Kazakh politics. This was especially evident when the capital of the country was moved to Almaty in the south. Both presidents, Dinmukhamed Kunayev and Nursultan Nazarbayev, belong to the Great Horde.

Most Russians in Kazakhstan live in the north, where they are close to Russia. Moving the capital from Almaty in the south to Astana in the north-central region was partly designed to make the area more Kazakh-dominated. But the urban areas are still populated by more Slavs than Kazakhs. About 60% of Kazakhs live in the countryside. Kazakh cities grew more as a result of migration into the country than as a result of the movement of Kazakhs from the countryside to the cities.

SLAVS

Russians make up the largest minority group in Kazakhstan. Most of them live in the cities of the steppes and plains in the north. This area is also populated by other ethnic Slavs—Ukrainians, Germans, and Belorussians—Tatars, and Koreans. For the Russians especially, living in northern Kazakhstan means that Russia is just a day's drive away. The rest of the population is made up of the other major ethnic groups of Central Asia—Uzbeks, Tajiks, and Uighurs.

A Russian villager tending her garden.

The Russians began their invasion of Central Asia in the late 16th century, establishing small forts along the way and completing their advance eastward to the Pacific Ocean by the middle of the 17th century. Russian traders and soldiers arrived on the northeast edge of the Kazakh territory in the 17th century, when Cossacks established the forts that later became the cities of Oral and Atyrau. The Russian takeover was made easier when the Kazakhs, pressured by the threat of invasions from China in the east, allied themselves with the Russian Empire.

The Russian soldiers were followed by Russian settlers. They cultivated the land and formed settlements around the forts. During the 19th century, there was a flood of immigrants to the region. About 400,000 Russians arrived, followed by about a million others, including Slavs, Germans, and Jews, who arrived during the first part of the 20th century.

Another large influx of Russians and Slavs occurred between 1954 and 1956 during the Virgin and Idle Lands project that was initiated by Nikita Khrushchev. These people settled in the rich agricultural areas in the north.

A Chechen refugee boy plays with his infant sister as other refugees gather in a room of a private house in Almaty.

"PROBLEM" PEOPLE

Between 1935 and 1940, Russia deported about 120,000 Poles from other areas of the Soviet Union to Kazakhstan. During World War II, the Soviet leader Stalin used Kazakhstan as a dumping ground for many groups of people that the Soviets regarded as "problems." The Germans who lived in the Volga region of the Soviet Union were deported because it was feared that they might help the enemy, Nazi Germany, although Germans had actually lived in the Volga region for almost two centuries. Nevertheless, their loyalty to the Soviet Union was in question. They were sent to Kazakhstan and Siberia with little food to sustain them.

The Tatars were another group of people to be deported during the war. The Tatars were people who were descended from the Mongols and had settled in the Crimean region. Stalin was afraid that they too might help the invading German army because they had suffered under the Soviet policy of collectivization. But Nazi Germany invaded the region before the Tartars could be deported. When the Soviet Union won the war and recaptured the Crimea, the Tatars were deported to Uzbekistan and Kazakhstan as punishment. Their villages in the Crimea were destroyed and all evidence of their culture erased. The Tatars claim that as many as 110,000 of their people died by 1946.

Since independence, non-Kazakhs have left Kazakhstan, going to other former Soviet republics. Many of them are technicians and skilled workers. At the same time, the government encourages Kazakhs from China and other parts of the former Soviet Union to return to their country. As a result of an uncertain future in Mongolia, Kazakhs there have also returned. They are welcomed by the government and are provided with housing, plots of land, and tax exemptions for two years.

ETHNIC TENSIONS

Independence has increased tension between the country's two largest ethnic groups: the Kazakhs and the Slavs. Slavs feel they are now at a disadvantage compared to the Kazakhs in terms of job opportunities and promotions. Although there are Slavic ministers in the government, many Slavs feel they will do better if they emigrate to the other CIS countries, especially Russia. The Slavs see Kazakhstan as a multi-ethnic home, therefore they want to enjoy equal status with the Kazakhs. On the other hand, Kazakhs see their independence as a rightful claim of their homeland, which the Russians invaded and dominated for a long time.

These people are among the 13.7% of the population who are unemployed in Kazakhstan (1998 estimate).

DISTRIBUTION OF THE POPULATION

Although Kazakhstan is the fourth most heavily populated of the former Soviet republics, its overall population density is low. In 1996, with a total population of 17,575,000, the population density was 17 per square mile (6 per square km).

The distribution of the population throughout the country is not even. Most people live in the cities. The urban areas are populated by more Slavs than Kazakhs. About 43% of Kazakhs live in the rural areas. About half of the inhabitants of Almaty, which until 1997 was the capital city, are Kazakhs. The cities have been created more as a result of the immigration of foreigners rather than because of a movement of Kazakhs from the country into the cities.

LIFESTYLE

THE IMPORTANCE OF THE FAMILY, respect for elders, and the responsibilities of belonging to a network of kinfolk and the clan are enduring values passed down through many generations of nomads, giving a Kazakh his or her identity. Although many modern Kazakhs, especially those who live in the cities, have never led a nomadic lifestyle, they are proud of this tradition.

THE NOMADIC LIFESTYLE

A nomad's life is essentially a difficult one. Each tribe has a hereditary route of migration and campsites that they use every year when they move their herds from winter to summer grazing. No group is allowed to use the grazing lands of another.

Left: **Kazakh nomads live in dome-shaped tents called** *yurts.* **These are made from flexible frameworks of willow wood covered with layers of felted wool for warmth. An opening at the top allows smoke from the central stove to escape. Opening and closing the vent allows occupants to control the temperature in the** *yurt.*

Opposite: **Early each morning, nomads bring their herds to the grazing grounds.**

The women take care of household chores such as washing and cooking, while the men look after the herds.

Nomads live at their main campsite during the winter. They normally spend four to five months a year there. The site is carefully chosen—it has to be sheltered and have ample water and grazing opportunities. Once they arrive at the campsite, they build their *yurts*, which are tent-like structures, or in some cases, create shelters from mounds of dirt, sticks, and stones.

Winter is a period of rest. Being in one area for a few months allows the nomads to make clothes and other items that they will need during the long trek back to their summer camp.

Once the snow melts and the new grass begins to grow, the nomads begin the spring migration to their summer campsites. Travel is slow, as they stop every few days and set up camp wherever there is a source of water. They proceed in this fashion until they reach their summer camp, usually by May or June.

On reaching the summer pastures, the group divides into smaller units and spreads out so that their animals have a greater area for grazing. When they break up into smaller units, "runners" carry messages between the groups. During the summer, the campsite might be moved several times within the general area if the grass or water becomes exhausted. The nomads remain at this campsite until August or September when all groups reassemble for the long trek back to their winter site.

The distances that the nomads cover during their migration varies from region to region: anything from 124 to 186 miles (200 to 300 km) in the south to as much as 621 miles (1,000 km) in the western and central parts of the country.

Each Kazakh household has its own herd, but the animals graze together with the herds of other households. Kazakhs own both sheep and goats, which they value very much, because sheep and goats provide them with food and clothing. They are also easy to feed as they eat all kinds of grass. But the animal that the Kazakhs truly treasure is the horse. It is the horse that makes their nomadic lifestyle possible. They can ride their horses and use them to carry household possessions. The central and southern Kazakhs often use camels instead of horses. Cattle were more commonly used in the north.

The nomads' biggest problem is the weather. If the winter is harsh, their animals will starve, especially if storms cover the grass with ice that is impenetrable. Kazakhs call this phenomenon a *jut* ("JART"). *Juts* occur about once every 10 to 12 years. In the summer drought is a problem. The nomads dig shallow wells along their migration routes, and these can dry up in years when there is little rain. The salinity of the lakes and rivers on the steppes are an additional problem. As a result of this harsh and demanding life, family relationships become very important as people have to depend on each other for survival.

Although some Kazakhs are farmers, this occupation is not much respected because farmers deprive the pastoralists of their grazing lands.

WAY OF THE ELDERS

Age is a positive attribute and one that is associated with wisdom. Kazakhs show great respect for their elders. This is one of the binding elements of Kazakh society and is known as "the way of the elders." Elders are treated with honor and deference whenever they are present, whether at home or elsewhere. Elders are always consulted to advise, to solve problems, and to make decisions that everyone respects and obeys. In the past it was imperative to obey an elder, and anyone who did not do so was punished. In this way the social structure is maintained. The same kind of deferential attitude shown to an elder is also shown to someone seen to be in a higher social position, such as a doctor or a teacher. A student would never criticize a teacher, nor would a junior worker criticize a supervisor.

Kazakh women are treated with as much respect as elder persons because they take good care of their family and home.

MARRIAGE TIES

In the past girls married at 13 or 14 and the men one or two years older. Today, however, the bride and groom have to be 18 years of age and both have to agree to the marriage. The engagement ceremony involves the groom's parents visiting the bride's parents to discuss a payment for the bride and her dowry. The dowry includes new clothes for the bride, a carpet, bed linen, and other household items, and a big trunk to hold these items. The payment depends on the wealth of the groom's family and is often paid in livestock. It can range from a few hundred sheep, camels, horses, and cows to several thousand cattle. If the bride's family agrees to the amount, the groom's father gives her father earrings and owl's feathers. Five or six relatives of the groom then visit the bride's father for a meal. The father gives each of them an animal as a sign of goodwill. The groom and his parents also give the bride's parents and relatives presents on the wedding day. Sometimes, thousands of guests are invited to the wedding.

A wedding ceremony in a church. Most Kazakh men have just one wife. It is rare today for a man to have two wives.

RIGHTS OF INHERITANCE

Each of the three hordes is subdivided into patrilineal lines. When a man dies, he passes on the family responsibility to his eldest son, and his herds are divided among all his sons.

Women do not have a share of the inheritance. The exceptions are an unmarried daughter, who gets part of the livestock; and a widow, who takes charge of the livestock if her sons are still too young. Although women have no inheritance rights, they are strong members of the society and are consulted on all matters of importance.

If a man dies without having any children, his possessions are returned to his father, who is obliged to look after his daughter-in-law. If not, her husband's brother has to take care of her, but only with her consent. If a widow remarries, her children remain with their father's family.

Boys learn sheep-herding from their father and uncles from the time they are young.

NETWORKING

As a result of the ties of marriage and kinship, a Kazakh man can always count on having the support of his relatives. He knows he can draw on the resources and the network of his relatives in times of need. He has three networks of relatives—his father's relatives, his mother's relatives, and his wife's relatives.

It is not unusual for a Kazakh living in the city to have his distant cousin suddenly arrive from the countryside for a visit. He is obliged to provide a meal and even a bed for his relative, who usually comes with gifts.

These obligations are extended to include a whole network of relationships, so a Kazakh may also call on the services and help of old friends, schoolmates, and fellow workers. The bigger and stronger a family's social connections are, the more favors can be requested. This is useful when a family member needs to get a job, obtain a permit, bypass some government regulation, obtain medical services, get a discount for a purchase, or send a child to university.

Friends and relatives are often obliged to join in the wedding celebrations of a couple. They are generally more than happy to share their joy.

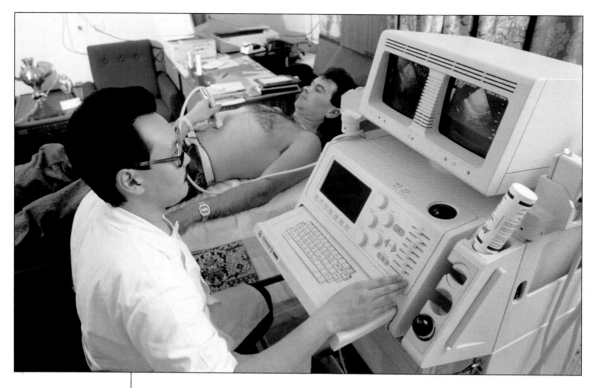

A medical diagnostic center in Karaganda.

HEALTH AND SOCIAL WELFARE

Kazakhstan had a well-established public health system that provided free medical care not only in the cities but also in the remote regions. This was a legacy from the Soviet system. However, the difficult years that immediately followed independence affected this public health service. The main problem is a lack of funds.

In 1993, in terms of medical systems, pharmaceutical supply, research and development, and medical sanitation, Kazakhstan was rated below average among the former Soviet republics. A poor diet, environmental pollution, and inadequate healthcare services are reasons for this. Life expectancy is also low compared with the West. The average lifespan of Kazakh men is 58 years, and 69 for women.

The 1995 constitution guarantees free, basic healthcare, although patients may have to pay for bandages and anesthesia. Besides public clinics, there are private medical services, but they are not allowed to treat patients with cancer, tuberculosis, and venereal and infectious diseases.

In 1992 the government spending on healthcare services was 1.6 % of the country's GDP (gross domestic product), an amount that classified it as an underdeveloped nation. The lack of funds has meant that doctors, nurses, and other medical personnel are paid very little and that sometimes, these already low wages are not paid. As a result, many people in the medical profession have left Kazakhstan for other republics, and strikes by doctors and nurses are not uncommon.

Since the 1990s, the declining birth rate has become a matter of state concern, and Kazakh nationalist parties have tried to ban birth control and abortions. In 1995 Nazarbayev stated that one of the country's goals is to create a society in which a woman is encouraged to work at home and raise her children. However, this makes it difficult for women to rise to senior positions in government or private enterprises, despite the fact that the constitution of 1995 safeguards against discrimination of all kinds.

A blind worker walks to his desk in a textile plant in Talgar, near Almaty. The factory employs about 170 blind workers.

EDUCATION

Education is mandatory and free through secondary school. Before independence, Russian was the only official language. After independence, Kazakh also became an official language. In the early 1990s schools continued to teach in Russian because there was a shortage of Kazakh textbooks and teachers. With increasing emphasis on Kazakh, more Russians are sending their children to Russia for their education. Local teachers are required to have a fluent knowledge of Kazakh, and this has led to more Kazakh than Slav teachers in primary and secondary schools.

There are 8,500 pre-schools in the country, as well as 8,757 elementary and secondary schools, which cover grades 1 to 12. After secondary education, students may choose to go to a college or university. Others may choose vocational training schools.

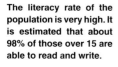

The literacy rate of the population is very high. It is estimated that about 98% of those over 15 are able to read and write.

Students attending computer class.

There was a reorganization of the school curriculum and changes in the textbooks after independence. Kazakh history, culture, and literature is getting greater attention. This has an effect not only in schools, but also in institutions of higher learning. The Kazakhstan Academy of Sciences has renewed its focus on matters that are of importance to the country, in the disciplines of the sciences and the humanities. Many research papers once considered incompatible with communist ideology have now been published either for the first time or for the first time after many years of being out of print.

Private education is allowed but is closely supervised and controlled by the state. More than 90% of children of primary and secondary school age attend school, but few proceed on to post-secondary education. Nevertheless, Kazakhstan has two established universities. The larger is the Al-Farabi State National University in Almaty. The smaller, second university is the Karaganda (Qaraghandy) State University. There are technical and secondary schools in five cities, including Almaty. In 1994, Kazakhstan had 32 specialized institutions of higher learning.

RELIGION

KAZAKHSTAN IS MAINLY A MUSLIM COUNTRY. Forty-seven percent of the population, mostly Kazakhs, belong to this religion. Despite the importance of Islam in the society, it is not the national religion. The 1995 constitution states that Kazakhstan is a secular state and protects religious freedom. Kazakhstan is the only state in Central Asia that does not give Islam special status.

ARABS BRING ISLAM

Islam was introduced to the area in the eighth century when the Arabs invaded the southern part of the country. However, many of the nomads did not become Muslims until the 18th century. The religion was practiced more by those who lived in the cities, mostly the traders, than by the pastoral people who had little knowledge of Islam's teachings and practices. The nomads' contact with Islam probably came from the holy men who traveled the steppes, following the Silk Road. Since they did not understand Arabic, they could not gain direct knowledge of the teachings of the Koran ("KOH-ran"), the holy book of the Muslims.

This change to Islam was not a difficult one because before Islam, Kazakhs believed in one god that they called Taingir. Since their ancient beliefs did not conflict with the new religion, the two merged easily and Islam became their new faith. In areas where Islam conflicted with the animistic and shamanistic beliefs, the ancient practices were abandoned without much concern.

Islam had a greater influence on people's lives after they moved into settlements and sent their children to school. Children were sent to Muslim schools and were taught the precepts of Islam and its ideology.

Above: A 19th-century Koran.

Opposite: Kazakh Muslims praying in a mosque. They pray five times a day.

Listening to the teachings of the Muslim *imam* **("ee-MAHM") or religious leader.**

But when Kazakhstan became part of the communist Soviet Union, all forms of religion were discouraged. This policy lasted for several decades until 1991, when the Soviet Union fell apart. Under the communists and when there was active repression of religion, many Kazakhs, though Muslims, never visited a mosque or read the Koran. During the late 1920s and the 1930s, the Soviet government became extremely anti-religion. Religious leaders were seen as influential figures, especially in the countryside, and the authorities wanted to get rid of them so that people would remain loyal only to the communist regime. The government closed down the mosques and religious schools and organizations and arrested the clergy. Nevertheless, the Muslim clerics continued to operate underground, and the people continued to sympathize with their religious leaders. After independence, the religious climate improved significantly. Kazakhstans generally are now free to practice any religion.

ISLAM'S FIVE PILLARS

Islam, Christianity, and Judaism have prophets in common. The Biblical patriarch, Abraham, had two sons, Isaac and Ishmael. Arabs believe they are descendants of Ishmael, while Jews are descendants of Isaac. Muslims believe God sent many prophets to teach the people—Abraham, Moses, David, Jesus, and Mohammed—and that Mohammed was the most important and last of the prophets. God (Allah) also sent the angel Gabriel to reveal his message to the people, and his words are written in the holy book called the Koran.

A true Muslim must follow the Five Pillars of Islam—the *shahadah* ("sha-HAHD-ah"), the declaration in Arabic that there is only one God, Allah, and that Mohammed is the messenger of Allah; prayer or *salat* ("sa-LAHT"); giving alms or *zakat* ("zah-KART"); fasting or *sawm* ("sa-AHM"); and going on pilgrimage or *hajj* ("HAHJ"). Giving alms, the third pillar, is intended to help the poor. Muslims give *zakat* once a year to the mosque or a Muslim welfare organization. Fasting is observed for the whole of Ramadan, which is the ninth month of the Islamic calendar. Muslims consider this the holy month. During this month, Muslims are not allowed to eat, drink, smoke, or have sex during the day. At night, they may resume these normal activities. Finally, a pilgrimage is required at least once in a person's lifetime to the holy city of Mecca. This is the *hajj*.

In addition, at all times of the year, Muslims are not allowed to eat pork or drink alcohol, gamble, or be unkind to others. They also have to say their daily prayers. Muslims must pray five times a day—before dawn, at noon, in the mid-afternoon, after sunset, and before going to bed. When it is time to pray, a man called the *muezzin* ("moo-EZ-in") calls the people to pray. His voice can be heard coming from the mosque five times a day. Muslims bow and face Mecca when they pray. On Fridays, they must go to the mosque for prayers. It is mostly the men who pray at the mosque. When women go, they have a separate place in which to pray. Muslim prayers are usually said in Arabic.

ISLAM IN KAZAKHSTAN TODAY

Although government statistics state that as many as 47% of the population claim to be Muslims, a large number of these people actually do not follow the precepts of their professed religion. This could be because they once followed a nomadic lifestyle, with little need for a central religious force. Truly staunch and practicing Muslims make up a very small percentage of the population. Most Kazakhs are just nominally Muslim and do not go to pray at the mosque. They may celebrate the Muslim festivals, but these celebrations have greater social than religious significance. Only those Kazakhs who are devout and able to afford it go on pilgrimages to Muslim holy places in Central Asia or Saudi Arabia.

The interior of a mosque. As a sign of respect, Muslims have to remove their shoes before entering a mosque.

ORTHODOX CHRISTIANS AND OTHERS

The other dominant religion in the country is the Russian Orthodox Church. Most of the Orthodox Christians are Russians, Ukrainians, and other Slavs. They make up about 44% of the population. The main church in Almaty is St. Nicholas Cathedral. There are also Protestants, mainly Baptists, as well as some Roman Catholics, Jews, and others.

THE EASTERN ORTHODOX CHURCH

The Eastern Orthodox Church is one of the three main branches of Christianity. The other two are the Roman Catholic Church and the Protestant Church. Today the Orthodox Church is made up of many local and national churches, each of which has a head called the patriarch. The major churches are in Greece, Russia, Eastern Europe, and western Asia.

The Church believes that it is faithful to the teachings of the Apostles of Christ and that it is free from errors in doctrinal matters. Orthodox churches are beautifully decorated with many religious images called icons. Easter is the most important time of the year, and every Sunday is considered a celebration of Christ's resurrection from the dead.

Orthodox Christians go to church every Sunday and on feast days. The church services are sung or chanted, and people usually stand during the services. There are several times during the year that fasts are observed. During these periods, the believer is not allowed to eat meat or dairy products, and sometimes not even fish. Devout people also fast every Wednesday and Friday.

ANCIENT PRACTICES

Most Kazakhs did not adopt Islam as a religion until the 18th century, and it was not strongly enforced or practiced by those who continued to live a nomadic life. Many nomads continue to observe pre-Islamic religious practices—shamanism, animism, and ancestor worship. These three practices are interrelated. Since the Kazakhs are pastoral and nomadic, it is easy to understand why they hold these beliefs. Their lifestyle and well-being are dependent on the weather and having healthy animals. Kazakhs believe that various animals, the earth, and celestial bodies like the sun and the moon are inhabited by the spirits of the dead. They also believe that there is a struggle for power between the forces of good and evil. When they embraced Islam, Prophet Mohammed and his teachings became the embodiment of the force of good.

Unlike Muslims in the Middle East countries, Kazakh Muslims are more informal about their Islamic beliefs.

In animism, different spirits are believed to inhabit animals. For the Kazakhs, these are the animals they are close to—sheep, cows, horses, and camels. Spirits are also present in the elements of fire, water, and earth, and may be contacted and asked for help. The nomads offer prayers to the water spirit in times of drought, to the earth spirit to ensure good weather, and to the animal spirits when the health of their livestock is threatened.

The shaman or medicine man is a wise person with special powers. He is able to mediate between the spirits and the people. Kazakhs are superstitious and will wear charms of holy objects to ward off evil spirits. They believe that it is possible to cast an evil eye on somebody you hate in order to hurt him. Trips to the graves of holy people and ancestors are made to ask for advice or to receive a blessing.

Because the traditional lifestyle is based on the rearing of animals, many customs and beliefs relate to livestock. When someone wishes another person ill, he will curse ill-health on the other person's livestock. For instance, a Kazakh might curse an enemy in this manner: "May you never own your livestock and be unable to migrate with your people," or "May you have neither horse nor camel, but always have to travel on foot." In the same way, blessings are expressed as an abundance of animals or a wish for their successful fertility. A Kazakh wishing someone well might offer this blessing, "May God bless you with one thousand sheep and lambs." When Kazakhs greet one another, it is good manners to inquire after the health of the other person's animals, for example, "Are you and your livestock healthy?"

Snow camels are sometimes kept on farms. Kazakhs believe spirits live in the bodies of the animals they are constantly in contact with.

RELIGIOUS CLIMATE TODAY

Since independence there has been an increase in religious activity. All religious groups have gained a new freedom to practice. Many more people now claim to be religious, and there is an increase in the number of religious organizations in the country.

Some groups that were illegal during Soviet times, such as Jehovah's Witnesses and several fundamentalist Christian groups, have been allowed into the country.

Islam is becoming increasingly important in modern Kazakh society. A number of mosques and religious schools have been constructed with financial aid from the Muslim countries of Saudi Arabia, Turkey, and Egypt. But while the Nazarbayev government is aware of the potential foreign investment it may receive from the Muslim countries of the Middle East, it has been careful to maintain a balance between the Muslim East and the Christian West. When President Nazarbayev made a trip to the Muslim holy city of Mecca in 1994, he also visited the Roman Catholic primate, Pope John Paul II, in the Vatican.

From 1985 to 1990 the number of mosques more than doubled from 25 to 60. An Islamic institute has been opened in Almaty. Since

1990 there has been an explosion of mosque building: there are now some 4,000 mosques believed to be functioning in the country. Loudspeakers on mosques broadcast the call to prayer five times a day and thus can be heard more and more in Kazakh cities.

Even President Nazarbayev makes occasional references to Allah in his speeches. Nevertheless, the state remains secular, that is, there is no official state religion. This is probably helpful in a country such as Kazakhstan where there are so many ethnic communities other than Kazakhs. The other communities might feel imposed on and would be extremely sensitive to any signs of a government favoring a dominant culture and religion.

Left: **Women praying in an Orthodox church.**

Opposite: **Stalls selling religious souvenirs set up by nuns to raise funds for their church.**

LANGUAGE

KAZAKH AND RUSSIAN ARE THE TWO OFFICIAL languages in Kazakhstan. Kazakh was declared the official language of the country in 1989, but the 1995 constitution recognized Russian as another official language. Kazakhstan is different from the other Central Asian republics of the CIS in that the majority of its people speak Russian. Only about forty percent of all Kazakhs speak their own language. About a third of the other Turkic-speaking people—the Uzbeks, Tatars, and Uighurs—also speak Kazakh while fewer than 10% of the rest of the population—Russians, Ukrainians, Belorussians, Koreans, and Germans—have bothered to master Kazakh. Russian is commonly used in business and communication. It is also the language of instruction in higher institutions, and parents prefer to send their children to schools that teach in Russian, to prepare them for higher education.

Left: **Though service is poor, telephones are available in most of Kazakhstan.**

Opposite: **The signboard of an entrepreneur's society in Almaty.**

When Kazakhstan became independent, the language problem became a contentious one. President Nazarbayev has tried to make Kazakh the only official language in the hopes of ensuring its survival as a language. But Russians in the country are afraid that it might lead to discrimination against them if Kazakh should become the only legal state language. There is the danger that a strong Kazakh language policy will cause skilled Russians, Slavs, and Germans to leave the country. But while most adult non-Kazakhs will probably not have to learn the language, the next generation of non-Kazakhs will be expected to learn Kazakh. The parliament has approved a new language law that requires all Kazakh citizens to learn Kazakh by the year 2006.

Workers who use computers must master the use of both Cyrillic and Roman alphabets on the keyboard.

KAZAKH

Kazakh became a written language in the 1860s. In 1929 the Latin, or Roman, script was introduced, and in 1940 Cyrillic script was used. Initiated by Josef Stalin, this alphabet unified the written language of the Soviet Central Asian republics with that of Russia. Modified in 1954, the 42-alphabet script now uses 33 letters of the standard Russian alphabet and some symbols specific to the Kazakh language. With independence, Kazakhstan has toyed with the idea of reintroducing the Latin-based alphabet, but this idea has been shelved because of the huge costs involved.

Kazakh is a Turkic language with strong Tatar and Mongol influences. It is part of the Nogai-Kipchak subgroup of northeastern Turkic languages.

Kazakh has several dialects; the main ones are Northeastern Kazakh, Southern Kazakh, and Western Kazakh. These dialects are quite similar to each other.

ORIGIN OF KAZAKH

The word "Kazakh" was found in a Turkish-Arabic dictionary in 1245. It means "independent, free, wanderer, exile," and refers to a free person who broke away from his people to lead the life of an adventurer or a group of nomads. The nomads in Kazakhstan were originally called Uzbek-Kazakhs as they were members of the Uzbek tribe who had broken away from the group. They began to drop the word "Uzbek" after 1468 when groups of Uzbek-Kazakhs united in victory from the Uzbek tribe. Burunduk Khan (1473–1511) was called the ruler of the "Kazakhs."

THE MEDIA

The main official newspapers in Kazakhstan are the Russian-language *Kazakstanskaya Pravda*, the organ of the Council of Ministers, and *Sovety Kazakstana*, the organ of parliament.

There are many other newspapers, and while these enjoy a certain amount of freedom and expression, guaranteed in the 1995 constitution, the government is increasing control over what is being published, while not engaging in outright censorship.

Some private newspapers have been refused publishing facilities at the government presses for various "technical" reasons, and sponsors of erring newspapers have faced investigations or had financial pressure brought on them. The law explicitly forbids any personal criticism of the president or his family.

In 1989 there were more than 450 officially registered newspapers being published in Kazakhstan. Of these, 160 were in the Kazakh language. There are also newspapers in other languages—Russian, Ukrainian, Uighur, German, English, and Korean.

Several newspapers have political links. The *Respublika* was published by the Socialist Party until it was sold to a commercial enterprise. The *NKK* is the paper of the People's Congress Party.

The largest independent newspaper, the *Panorama*, is owned by some of the largest businesses in the country. The newspaper tries to focus an objective eye on political and economic issues. Two other purely commercial newspapers are the tabloid *Karavan* and the *Almaty Business News*. Both are published by a Russian-owned company, called Karavan.

Radio and television are extremely important in linking the distant parts of the country together. Besides the national broadcasting service, foreign broadcasting stations in the neighboring countries of Uzbekistan and Kyrgyzstan together with Moscow stations give Kazakh listeners more choices in television programs.

A television tower in Almaty. There are 20 television broadcast stations in Kazakhstan; eight of them are government-owned, while the rest are private stations.

ARTS

KAZAKH CULTURE IS RICHLY ENDOWED with fine arts such as painting and sculpture, as well as music, theater, and literature. In addition, it has a well-established and important tradition of oral history through which modern Kazakhs have been able to maintain their link with the past.

ORAL TRADITIONS

Before the mid-19th century, most Kazakh customs and traditions were part of an oral tradition of stories and poetry. Storytellers and singers, called *akyns* ("A-keens"), and lyric poets, known as *jyrau* ("JAI-rau"), were entrusted with the responsibility of memorizing the stories, legends, and history of the Kazakh people and keeping these cultural history alive by reciting it and passing it on to the next generation of storytellers.

Left: Dancers in traditional costume.

Opposite: The creativity of Kazakhs is also apparent in the architecture of their buildings.

The statue of a famous *akyn*, Jambyl. This statue, situated in Almaty, was sculpted by a well-known Kazakh artist called Khakimzhan Naurzbayev.

Akyns are storytellers who traveled from one nomadic camp to another reciting the epic stories of Kazakh history and legend. Many of the stories tell of the exploits of legendary warriors and their struggle against Mongol Kalmyks. The stories are often told to the accompaniment of traditional instruments such as the drum. The Kalmyks were pastoral nomads and descendents of the Mongols who lived in the eastern and southeastern parts of the country. They fought the Kazakhs for control of the land in the 17th century.

But not all stories tell of battles or warrior heroes. Some are romantic tales, such as the love story of Enlik and Kebek, who chose death in the face of family opposition to their love, while others, such as the most famous love story, *Kiz-Jibek*, are lyrical love poems.

The poems and poetic songs of the khanate period survived because they were preserved orally until the late 19th century, when they were recorded by Kazakh intellectuals. But the Soviets suppressed these records until the 1960s.

The *jyrau* are respected members of their tribes and honored as elders. They are often part of the ruler's retinue of followers. Unlike the *akyns*, the *jyrau* have contact with the world at large, and their poetry contains Islamic elements with references to Allah.

One famous poet is Asan Kangi, who lived from 1370 to 1465. He served the Mongolian court of the Golden Horde. Other notable poets are Dosbambet-Jhyrau (1490–1523) and Jhalkiz Jhyrau (1465–1560).

MUSICAL TRADITION

Music plays an equally big role in Kazakh life, complementing the oral tradition of storytelling. It is a means of entertainment, and no festival is complete without a band of musicians playing. But, together with storytelling, music is also a way of recording tribal history in song, and it has magical qualities when it is employed by the shaman or medicine man.

The nomads used songs and instrumental music called *kyuis* to pass on their traditions from one generation to the next. For example, each seasonal migration was blessed by a special song sung by an elder, called the *aksakal*.

A folk orchestra performing in the national theater.

There are more than 50 Kazakh musical instruments—string, wind, and percussion. They are made from wood, metal, reed, leather, horn, and horsehair. The most common string instruments that Kazakhs play are the two-stringed, lute-like instrument called a *dombra* and the *komuz*, another lute-like instrument with three strings. Some older lutes have strings that are made of horsehair and others of silk. The *kobyz* is like a violin; its body is made of one piece of wood and the strings are played with a bow. Another string instrument is the *zhetigen*, which has a rectangular wooden body and seven strings made of horsehair. It is used mainly as a solo instrument or as an accompanying instrument in folk orchestras and ensembles.

Young children learning national music. They are playing the *dombra*.

Musical Tradition

The *sybyzgy* is a wind instrument. Commonly used by traditional musicians, it is made of reed or wood and resembles two small wooden flutes put together. The *adyrna* is also a wind instrument. Although basically a musical instrument, hunters often use it because in skilful hands the whistle-like sound of the *adyrna* resembles the cries of birds and other animals.

There are several percussion instruments. The *dangyra* is similar to the tambourine. One side is covered with leather, and the inner rim of the instrument is lined with metal pendants that produce clacking sounds when the instrument is struck. Two drum-like instruments are the *dauylpaz* and the *dabyl*. Both are beaten with the hand or a whip and are often used for signaling in the army and for hunting.

The *asatayak* is used in shamanistic rituals. It is a wooden staff or rod about 3 feet (1 m) long with metal pendants at the top. When shaken, it produces a rattling sound.

Traditional Kazakh folk singers often accompany their performances on the *dombra* or *kobyz*. There are many traditional folk songs that are sung on special occasions, such as the *koshtasu*, a song of farewell for close friends and family; the *yestirtu*, sung to announce the death of someone dear; the *zhoktau*, a song of lamentation; and the *konil aitu*, a song to comfort the grieved.

The Museum of Kazakh Musical Instruments in Almaty houses a unique collection of traditional Kazakh musical instruments. The museum also displays the personal musical instruments of Abay Kunanbayev and other famous Kazakh musicians. The wooden museum building itself is of artistic and historical interest. It is the achievement of the architect Andrei Zenkov, who built Zenkov Cathedral, another totally wooden building. The museum was built in 1907.

TEXTILES

Kazakh arts and crafts have a long tradition. The people are well known for their beautiful embroidery work on all types of daily and ceremonial articles, such as the velvet vest that is part of the Kazakh traditional dress.

Multicolored threads are combined with beads and stones to decorate items made of cloth, leather, felt, and other materials.

Carpet making is another tradition for which Kazakhs are famous. The northeastern part of the country is most well-known for this craft. Many Kazakh houses are decorated with handmade felt carpets and rugs of intricate colors and geometric designs.

The process of making a felt carpet is elaborate. It begins with the cleaning and dying of the wool. The dyed wool is then laid on a mat of hay and reeds (called *tchiy*) harvested from the steppes, wet down, and then walked on by everyone in the household. This trampling mats and fuses the wool fibers. The designs are then cut out of different colored felts and combined. This arrangement is then covered by the reed mat and stepped on again until the sections stick to each other. When the carpet is uncovered, the youngest daughter in the family sews everything together.

Carpets are a common sight in Kazakhstan, and people like to decorate their homes with colorful felt carpets.

SILVERSMITHING

Silversmithing as a Kazakh craft reached its height in the late 19th and early 20th centuries. The silversmiths were kept busy by the wealthy, who required jewelry to complement their ornate costumes. The designs of Kazakh jewelry are similar to those of other Central Asian societies, such as the Turkmen and Tatars. Plant and animal motifs are used widely, as are geometric patterns, including circles, triangles, and dots. The silversmiths are skilled in engraving. Intricate filigree is one of the hallmarks of fine Kazakh jewelry in which delicate lacy designs are created with gold and silver wire. Further ornamentation is achieved by making use of precious and semiprecious stones for color and detail. Saddles and stirrups are lovingly created and decorated with silverwork.

NATURE PAINTERS

Creativity remains a part of the Kazakh tradition to this day. The Union of Kazakhstani Artists is the country's largest artistic organization, gathering together more than 600 painters, sculptors, folk artists, craftspeople, and other creative people.

A nature painter in her gallery.

Popular subjects for artists are scenes from nature: landscapes, especially the steppes; the changing seasons; people in the city and in nomadic settings; and portraits of famous Kazakhs like Abay Kunanbayev.

Artists who have achieved distinction are awarded the title of "People's Artist of Kazakhstan." Of these, Abylkhan Kasteyev (1904–73) is well-known, being a pioneer of Kazakh painting. He painted idealized images of collectivization and the Virgin Lands program. Among his major works are the paintings *A Hunter with a Golden Eagle*, *An Alpine Skating Rink*, and *Summer Pasture of Chalkude*.

The interior of a museum in Akmola.

MUSEUMS AND THEATERS

Almaty is a lively center of Kazakh art and culture with many theaters and museums. The Abay Academic Opera and Ballet House, which was established in 1934, stages Kazakh operas and ballets, as well as Western productions like *Swan Lake*. There are also theaters that showcase the artistic traditions of other communities in the country—the M. O. Auszov Kazakh State Academic Russian Drama Theater was founded in 1926; M. Yu Lermontov State Academic Russian Theater was set up in 1933; G. Musrepar State Academic Theater for Youth and Children in 1944; N. Sats State Academic Russian Theater for Youth and Children in 1945; the Republican German Drama Theater in 1998; and the State Republican Uigur Theater of Musical Comedy in 1934. The Republican Korean Theater of Musical Comedy, originally formed in Vladivostok in 1932, arrived in Kzyl-Orda in 1937, when Koreans were deported by the Russians to Kazakhstan, and moved to Almaty in 1968.

Kazakhs are lovers of museums. The Central Museum in Almaty houses a permanent collection of archeological finds from all over the country, historical artifacts relating to ancient, modern, and natural history, and the history of the major ethnic communities in the country. There is an art museum with crafts, art, and paintings, an Archeology Museum, Geology Museum, Nature Museum, and even a Museum of Books.

The A. Kasteyev Museum of Fine Arts was established with a beginning collection of almost 200 art works by Russian and European artists in 1935. Today it has, in addition, a section of traditional Kazakh crafts, jewelry, and clothing, as well as to Chinese, European, and Kazakh paintings.

WRITERS

Abay Kunanbayev (1845–1904) is probably the most well-known literary figure in Kazakh history. He was born in the Chingiz-Tau Mountains, south of the town of Semey in northeastern Kazakhstan. Although Kunanbayev never left his native land, he was very well educated and knowledgeable about the world. He spoke several languages, among them Russian, Arabic, and Persian. Kunanbayev spent three years in an Islamic school, then taught, translated Russian literature into Kazakh, and wrote poetry. He was a nationalist who promoted Kazakh cultural identity. He spoke out strongly for the need to educate the young in order to create a moral and spiritual world. Kunanbayev idealized the traditional Kazakh life, while also advocating progress through collaborating with the Russians. Through his work, Kazakh earned its place as a literary language.

The great Kazakh poet, Abay Kunanbayev.

Mukhtar Auezov (1897–1961) was the son of a nomadic family. He was a writer, literary critic, historian, and linguist. Through his writings, he gave immortality to the life and culture of his people and country. He learned the power of the written word early in life. As a child, he was amazed to discover that Kazakh stories and songs could be written and preserved on paper. His greatest book is the epic called *The Path of Abay* or *Abay's Way*. In it, he explores in the life and philosophy of the poet Abay Kunanbayev, paying homage to the poet he revered above all others. Auezov died at the age of 64 in Moscow.

LEISURE

THE HORSE IS CENTRAL to the Kazakh traditional lifestyle, so it is not surprising that many leisure activities and sports have to do with the display of good horsemanship. Kazakhs are exceptional horsemen. Children learn to ride almost as soon as they can walk. Jumping onto a horse and riding out on the steppes is as commonplace as riding a bicycle around the block in America.

COURTSHIP GAME

There are a number of traditional games that Kazakhs play on horseback. One is a catch-me-if-you-can game of tag that boys and girls sometimes play. It is called *kyz kuu* ("KISS-ku") or "overtake the girl." When a boy catches a girl, he earns a kiss from her. But if the girl catches up with him, she gets to hit him with her riding whip.

Left: **The *kyz kuu* takes place at top speed on horseback out on the steppes.**

Opposite: **Kazakh men with their most-prized possessions—hunting eagles.**

KAZAKH POLO

Kokpar is a very popular game in Kazakhstan. It is a wild, free-for-all scramble by Kazakhs on horseback who fight for possession of the carcass of a goat. Perhaps the game that is most similar to *kokpar* is polo. The chase on horseback is the same, but ends there. Instead of a polo ball, the headless carcass of a goat is tossed around. As many as a thousand participants can take part in the chase. There are no boundaries; the action can extend out over the steppes. The game supposedly originated as a sacrificial tradition where a goat was killed in order to obtain the blessings of the spirits. After the game, there would be a grand feast and musical performances.

Celebrating the end of a *kokpar* with a song performance.

SILVER COIN TEST

Another time-honored game that tests one's horsemanship is *kumis alu*, which means "pick up the coin." The aim is for the rider to gallop at top speed and simultaneously pick up a silver coin from the ground. This game requires the participant to possess almost perfect riding skills. Kazakh folklore has it that Alexander the Great, after seeing an exhibition of *kumis alu*, was so impressed that he exclaimed the game could be used in the training of a warrior on horseback. In modern games, a white handkerchief is used instead of a coin.

WRESTLING

Kazakhs love wrestling. This sport has a strong Central Asian tradition, and a champion wrestler is an honored man. *Audaryspak*, or wrestling on horseback, pits both riders and their horses in close combat. The winner is the one who is able to unseat his opponent from his horse.

Two wrestlers in close combat. Wrestling, like *kokpar* and *kumis alu*, originated from the warrior tradition. In ancient times Kazakh tribes fought many battles, all on horseback. The games were a form of training for the soldiers.

A Kazakh hunter with his eagle and horse. Hunting does not stop even during the harsh winters.

BERKUTCHI

This is the sport of hunting with eagles for which Kazakhs are famous. *Berkutchi* is the name of the sport and also of the men who capture the eagles and teach them to hunt. Eagles are caught in a net trap that is baited with a small animal like a hare. When an eagle takes the bait and flies into the net, the hunter's first job is to tie the bird's legs together to immobilize its claws. Then a small leather hood is thrown over its eyes. This usually calms the bird. Then the patient job of training the bird starts.

The hood is kept on the eagle while it becomes accustomed to the sounds, touch, and presence of people. After a week, the bird is taught to take its food directly from its master's hand. As training progresses, the eagle is given more leeway and is allowed to fly. The bond between bird and master grows until finally the eagle can be released and trusted to return when called. It is trained to hunt with the use of stuffed foxes.

Berkutchi hunt for fox with an eagle, a hound, and a horse. They ride on the steppes in search of a fox. When one is spotted, the hunter takes off the leather hood covering the bird's eyes and launches the bird into the sky. As the eagle circles in the sky and then swoops down on its prey, the hunter follows closely on his horse. The eagle catches the fox in its strong talons. The hunter has to be quick to call his bird back, rewarding its success with some raw meat he keeps in a little leather pouch. The hood is quickly slipped back on to calm down the bird.

Hunters can earn good money by selling fox skins. Fox-hunting is a skill that is passed down from father to son, but it is a dying tradition today. Petroglyph drawings of men hunting with an eagle show that it is an ancient sport. Berkutchi believe that they have to keep their first kill for at least a year for good luck. One way is have the fox fur made into a handsome hat. Eagle-hunting competitions are held during festivals.

Besides golden eagles, hunters sometimes use hawks and falcons. They also hunt other birds such as partridge, duck, and pigeon, and animals such as hare and even wolves.

STORYTELLING

Storytelling is an important part of Kazakh tradition, going back to the days when the *akyn* or storyteller-cum-bard would journey from camp to camp to tell stories. The *akyn* would tell of the people's history or sing songs. Both adults and children looked forward to a visit from the *akyn*.

The stories were a means of remembering the history of the Kazakhs and of teaching social values. Many stories had morals to teach and were animal stories in which the animals were given human characteristics. In her book *Stories of the Steppes*, author Mary Lou Masey translates these Kazakh folktales. One story shows how a mouse, small but intelligent, is able to outwit bigger and stronger animals.

LEISURE TODAY

The Medey speed-skating rink, located near Almaty, is a symbol of the modernization of Kazakhstan. The world's largest ice-skating rink, Medey is an open-air stadium with a rink that is 1,313 feet (400 m) long. During the week, it is used by ice hockey teams and world-class speed skaters, but it is open to the public on Sunday. Hundreds of skaters can then be seen swirling and tumbling across the ice. It is the site for many international competitions, and more than 100 world skating records have been broken there.

Kazakhs enjoy a wide variety of outdoor activities like hiking, hunting, mountain climbing, and skiing. The town of Shymbulaq in the foothills of the Tien Shan range, near the city of Almaty, is one of Central Asia's premier ski resorts. The area is beautiful, filled with glaciers and lakes. Local residents and a growing number of tourists like to hike there.

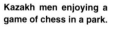

Kazakh men enjoying a game of chess in a park.

Hunting and fishing are also popular activities. Birds, such as the partridge and pheasant, fox, wolves, deer, and wild boar are all popular game. Fishing enthusiasts like to catch roach, carp, chub, and silverfish. A government licence is required for fishing and hunting.

The country also offers numerous spas that are popular with both residents and tourists. These holiday resorts offer guests all sorts of medicinal treatments with curative waters.

In Almaty's Panfilov Park, Kazakh men play chess in the shadow of Zenkov Cathedral. Chess is an extremely popular game among Central Asians and has been so for a very long time.

Kazakhs are becoming increasingly exposed to modern, Western culture. Movie theaters and television show American, Russian, Chinese, and Turkish movies. Rock concerts are not uncommon. The Manhattan Disco is Almaty's new hot spot where visitors and locals can dance under flashing lights to the latest Western tunes.

Horse racing is another popular pastime, especially during summer weekends at the race track in Almaty.

A pool of muddy water at a construction site can be lots of fun for creative Kazakh children.

FESTIVALS

PUBLIC HOLIDAYS IN KAZAKHSTAN are linked to social and political events. Because Kazakhstan is a former Soviet republic, many holidays have political significance. For instance, March 8 is International Women's Day, and Victory Day, on May 9, celebrates the end of World War II for Russia. There are no religious holidays. Nauryz, the traditional Central Asian celebration of spring, is a recent addition to the Kazakh calendar.

During the early Soviet era, Nauryz was illegal. Later, the Soviet authorities decided that Nauryz could be a non-religious festival that all Soviet people in Central Asia could enjoy.

Since independence in 1991, the Kazakh government has encouraged the celebration of Nauryz as an expression of the people's nationalistic pride. The festival is the people's link to their pre-Soviet past and symbolizes a revival of tradition.

Left: **Celebrating Christmas in church.**

Opposite: **A Kazakh artist holding a flaming cup during a Nauryz celebration in Almaty.**

CELEBRATION OF SPRING

Nauryz is probably the most important festival of the year, celebrated by everyone in Kazakhstan, regardless of ethnicity. It is a celebration of the coming of spring, the emergence of the first grain or sheaf of wheat, the lambing season, and the first milking. The festival is also called "the first day of the New Year" or "the great day of the people."

Symbols that are associated with Nauryz are the color white, which stands for goodness and riches; sweets, for abundance; and the number seven, which has a mystical significance. The traditional Nauryz dish is *kozhe*, made with seven kinds of grain, including rice, millet, and wheat. The elders of the family are ceremonially offered seven bowls of *kozhe*.

A carnival in the streets of Astana. The stalls sell food, drinks, and many interesting souvenirs.

ORIGINS OF NAURYZ

The celebration of Nauryz came to Kazakhstan through the influence of the nearby Persians many centuries ago. It is still celebrated in Iran, modern-day Persia, where it is called No Ruz or Norooz. The word in the Farsi or Persian language means "new day." In Kazakhstan Nauryz is a celebration of the coming of spring and the symbolic victory of good over evil. The first No Ruz was believed to have been celebrated by the legendary Persian emperor, Jamshid. Some historians think that it was celebrated as long ago as in the 12th century B.C. There are many similarities in the way the Iranians and Kazakhs celebrate this festival. Since Nauryz is a time for renewal, families clean their homes to remove the previous year's dust, open their homes to everyone, buy new clothes, and visit their friends. The number seven is also important—families have a table on which they place seven objects, each beginning with the letter "S"—*samanu*, a sweet made of flour and sugar; *sekeh*, a coin; *sabzee*, green vegetables; *sonbol*, a hyacinth flower; *seer*, garlic; *senjed*, a dried fruit; and *serkeh*, vinegar.

No effort is spared in this celebration since Kazakhs believe that the more one celebrates Nauryz, the greater will be one's reward and success for the rest of the year. A lot of cooking, especially of special dishes that symbolize abundance and good tidings, is done as people visit family and friends to wish them well in the coming year. It is important that there is more than enough food and drink for all.

Although Nauryz was originally a nonreligious celebration with Persian origins, it has been given a Muslim flavor in the southern part of the country. The celebrations are blessed by the Muslim *imam* and presided over by the elders of the community. Celebrations begin when the new year is greeted at noon with a prayer honoring the ancestors. This is read by the religious leader. Then the eldest in the family solemnly gives a blessing and wishes of prosperity and goodwill to everybody present.

Entertainment during Nauryz blends the modern with the traditional. In the cities Nauryz has a more secular nature. Processions, with horsemen dressing up as Kazakh heroic warriors, fill the streets, while wrestling competitions and horse races sizzle the air with excitement. Musicians perform to a lively audience, and folk singers engage in song battles.

The atmosphere during Nauryz resembles that of a carnival. In addition to the entertaining variety shows, there are stalls selling food and all kinds of merchandise.

An elderly Kazakh man prays with other Muslims to celebrate Eid al-Adha.

MUSLIM CELEBRATIONS

Kazakh Muslims, like their counterparts elsewhere, observe Ramadan, the ninth month of the Islamic year, and the feast of Eid al-Fitr, also called Little Bairam or the Festival of the Breaking of the Fast, which marks the end of Ramadan. The next important Muslim celebration is Eid al-Adha, also called the Great Festival or the Festival of the Sacrifice. However, neither of these two big Muslim celebrations are national holidays in Kazakhstan.

Islam follows the lunar calendar, and therefore the feasts are "movable," that is, the dates change from year to year. The first day of the month is determined by the observation of the moon by the religious authority. When the new moon of the ninth month is sighted, Ramadan begins. The holy month ends when the next new moon is seen.

During Ramadan, Muslims fast from sunrise to sunset, abstaining from food, drink, and tobacco, although they still carry on their normal activities. When the month is over, the end of Ramadan is celebrated with the feast of Eid al-Fitr, which usually lasts for three days. During this time, everyone's house is open to all friends and family. People go visiting, and there is a lot to eat and drink. Although Muslims traditionally do not drink alcohol, many Kazakh Muslims are not strict on this point, and vodka is commonly served.

Eid al-Adha is the Feast of Sacrifice and celebrates the completion of a *hajj* or a holy pilgrimage to Mecca, which is the holy city for all Muslims. During Eid al-Adha, all Kazakhs who can afford to will kill an animal as a sacrifice and share it in a meal with others. Families and friends visit one another on this festival.

VOICE OF ASIA INTERNATIONAL MUSIC FESTIVAL

The Voice of Asia International Music Festival is one of the grandest festivals in Central Asia. Held in July or August every year, the festival's aim is to combine contemporary music with traditional folk music. The colorful festival attracts not only young Kazakh singers, but it also draws famous international pop stars to join the International Contest of Performers. The contest offers attractive cash prizes from $1,000 to $10,000. Another competition, the Contemporary Song of Kazakhstan contest, features the many beautiful compositions of contemporary Kazakh composers, sung by Kazakh singers. Besides these competitions, there are also a gala concert, a Festival of Oriental fashion, a Festival of Oriental Cuisine, and artists' exhibitions, and a Festival of Children's Art held at the same time.

The song festival used to be held in the Medey Ice-skating Stadium, in the mountains of Almaty. In 1997 and 1999, it was moved to the Almaty Summer Theater in the City Park.

The 11th Voice of Asia International Music Festival, from July 28 to August 1, 2000, was held in honor of an internationally acclaimed Kazakh opera singer, Yermek Serkebayev. He had been the leading singer at the Abay Opera and Ballet Theater for more than 50 years.

STATE FESTIVALS IN KAZAKHSTAN

New Year, Jan 1;
International Women's Day, March 8;
Nauryz, March 21;
Kazakhstan People's Unity Day, May 1;
Victory Day, May 9, which commemorates the end of World War II;
Constitution Day, August 30, which celebrates the adoption of the new constitution in 1995;
Republic Day, October 25; and
Independence Day, December 16, when Kazakhstan became independent from the Soviet Union in 1991.

A family having a meal together.

THE SIGNIFICANCE OF FEASTS

There are many events in a Kazakh's life that call for a feast. Births, deaths, marriages, significant birthdays—these are all celebrated with feasting, songs, and games. There are also many ceremonies for celebrating the special moments in a baby's life—when it is born, the first time it is placed on a bed, when it first stands, when it first walks, and when it is weaned.

Boys are often circumcised when they are between 5 to 8 years old. It is common for a boy to be circumcised with other boys, such as his brothers or cousins. There is usually a small gathering and celebration on the day of circumcision. Guests are invited to visit with the boys in the recovery room briefly to commend them on their courage and to congratulate them for taking this important step in their life. The boys also receive gifts, often a small sum of money. Then the guests are ushered into the living room where they are offered food and drink. The big celebration is usually reserved for a later date, about a month or so later.

The Significance of Feasts

Preparations for a celebration begin months before the actual date. Shopping trips to the nearest city are made to buy all the items needed. Wealthy families may travel to the big cities to buy special or hard-to-get foods and gifts. Invitations are printed and sent. Gifts for the guests are picked out and set aside.

Everyone in the family is involved in the preparation. Besides the members of the immediate family, the services of friends and members of the extended family are called on. If possible, the feast is held in the yard. Tables are set up and animals slaughtered. Food is cooked over several days.

On the big day itself, guests arrive with their gifts. Gifts can range from a small piece of clothing or jewelry to a camel or a horse. As the guests are shown to their seats, a master of ceremony begins to take charge of the events of the day. The table of honor is usually the one farthest away from the entrance. This is where the person whom the feast honors sits, together with other important guests. Everyone dresses in his or her best clothes, whether in traditional dress or in western dress and suits.

If it is a wedding, the bride and groom are ushered to their seats by dancers. If it is a circumcision ceremony, then the boy is brought to the guests to be congratulated.

The tables are loaded with drinks that usually include vodka, fermented mare's milk, and an endless flow of hot tea. Snacks of nuts, fruit, cookies, and candy keep everyone happy in between the main courses of soup, dumplings, pies, fried dough, and bread. Meat is present in every dish, and the richer the family, the more meat there will be.

Sometimes, a band is hired to provide some music while the guests dance. There may also be horse races and games, and the host presents prizes to the winners.

Although there was a suppression of Kazakh culture and tradition during Soviet times, the authorities could never really stop the feasts that accompanied the celebrations of life events in the community. Feasting and gift-giving have always had great cultural significance in Kazakh society. They create ties that bind people to one another.

FOOD

HOSPITALITY AND GENEROSITY are the trademarks of the Kazakh people. A guest, whether expected or not, is always given a cordial welcome and a place of honor, and however impoverished a kitchen, the best food will be set before a guest. From a young age, girls are trained in the art of making a guest welcome. Be it one person or many people, the Kazakh hostess does not balk at her task.

MEAT

Meat is the most important feature of any Kazakh dinner. Although Kazakhs eat a lot of mutton and beef, horse meat is prized above all and often reserved for very special dishes. Almost all parts of the animal are eaten, including the internal organs. The heads of sheep and horses are delicacies and offered to guests of honor.

Left: **When animals are slaughtered, the meat is usually preserved by salting, drying, or smoking.**

Opposite: **A fruit market in Almaty.**

The meat section of a busy indoor market in Almaty.

Kazy, *shuzhuk*, *zhaya*, *zhal*, and *karta* are all delicacies made from horse flesh. They are all either salted or smoked and boiled. *Kazy* is a sausage made of smoked meat taken from the horse's ribs. It is salted, peppered, spiced, and put into horse intestines that have been washed and cleaned in salt water. It is sometimes served sliced with cold noodles. *Shuzhuk* is another kind of dried or smoked sausage. *Zhaya* is made from the meat of the horse's hip. *Zhal* is the fat from the underpart of the horse's neck. *Karta* is made from the horse's rectum. It is carefully washed without removing the fat and turned inside out, dried, smoked, and salted.

Shashlyk, or kebabs, are pieces of mutton and fat skewered and barbecued over a charcoal stove. They are often sold at street stalls.

Fish and chicken are also part of the Kazakh diet but are not as important as beef, mutton, and horse meat. Fish comes mainly from the Caspian Sea and includes pike, perch, sprats, beluga, sturgeon, and salmon. It is usually boiled but is sometimes fried. Boiled chicken and fried fish can be served as cold appetizers before the main meat dish is presented. Caviar is a delicacy in Kazakhstan.

KAZAKH CUISINE

Kazakh cuisine is varied. Rice, vegetables and legumes, milk products, and bread are commonly eaten. Vegetables are always part of a meal, but they are seldom the main course. Radishes, carrots, potatoes, onions, peppers, and various types of green vegetables are often embellishments to meat dishes. Kazakhs like their food spiced and garnished with garlic, dill, parsley, and other herbs. *Plov* or *pilaf* is a rice dish and can be a simple concoction of rice, chopped mutton, and shredded vegetables fried in a large pan. A chef's version would be a fragrant combination of meat and rice, flavored with raisins and other dried fruit and the famous Kazakh apples. *Sorpa* is a soup flavored with meat or fish and served with flour dumplings or rice. *Kespe* is a soup made of meat or poultry and noodles. It is rather oily because Kazakhs love to eat the fatty parts of the meat.

Families that raise chickens also eat eggs, but they never serve them at important feasts because Kazakhs look on eggs as a poor substitute for meat.

FRIED AND FLAT BREAD

Kazakh bread is mainly in the form of flat cakes made with wheat flour, sometimes leavened with yeast. Some breads like the *taba-nan* are baked in an oven or buried in hot charcoal. *Baursak* is a bread dough that is fried in fat. These are eaten as snacks, with sour cream and sugar, or as an accompaniment to the main meat course. *Lepeshka* is a round, unleavened bread.

Millet is another important part of the Kazakh diet. It is either pounded or used whole. Kazakhs are very inventive in their methods of cooking millet: frying it in fat, boiling it in milk, or adding it to a meat and vegetable soup to create a nourishing broth.

A Kazakh woman with the different types of breads she has baked. Bread is a staple in the Kazakh diet.

MILK FOODS

A large and important part of Kazakh cuisine consists of food made of milk and milk products. Kazakhs use the milk of all their livestock—cows, sheep, camels, and goats. Those who live in the country are able to make their own butter, sour cream, yogurt, and cheese. In addition, they also produce many other kinds of dairy products.

The milk of an animal that has just had its young is called beestings. This milk is higher in protein and vitamins and lower in sugar and fats than milk produced later. Kazakhs differentiate three kinds of beestings. The milk immediately after calving is black beestings; the milk obtained after the calf has had its first feeding is yellow beestings, and the milk obtained 24 hours after calving is white beestings. Yellow beestings is mixed with milk, poured into a cleaned animal's stomach, and boiled with meat. White beestings is collected in a bucket, boiled, and drunk.

Irimshik is the dried curd made from the milk of a cow, sheep, or goat. Fresh milk is curdled by the addition of a rennet bag. (Rennet is the stomach of the animal that digests the curd that it chews.) The sour milk is then boiled over a low fire until the curds and whey are separated. The curd is then strained and dried in the wind and sun. It has an orange color. The whey can also be boiled slowly until a thick viscous mass is left at the bottom of the pot. This is cooled and dried in flat sheets, producing *sarysu*. *Sarysu* is sometimes called Kazakh chocolate because it supposedly tastes like chocolate.

A Kazakh boy eating a cheese snack made from cow's milk. Dried milk by-products are an important source of nourishment for Kazakh nomads when fresh food is unavailable.

Separating the cream from the milk, a task carried out by the nomad women every morning.

MILK DRINKS

Kazakhs make a number of drinks from the milk of their animals. Horse and camel milk are served at wedding feasts. *Kumys* is an alcoholic drink made from fermented mare's milk. It is a traditional drink of the nomads of Central Asia and is extremely popular. The time-honored way of making *kumys* is to put the mare's milk into a bag made of camel or goat skin, place it in a warm spot in the *yurt*, and allow the natural fermentation process to take place. This usually occurs within a day. The *kumys* is then beaten with a stick.

Shubat is fermented camel's milk. It is richer and fatter than *kumys*. *Shubat* is made in a similar manner, and it must be stirred. *Airan* is a kind of yogurt produced from sheep's, goat's, or mare's milk.

Kazakhs believe in the medicinal and curative qualities of these milk drinks. Besides nutritional value, the drinks are believed to cure a number of digestive and intestinal problems. It is a special honor to be offered any of these drinks, so that it would be a social error for a guest to refuse.

UNIVERSAL TEA

The drink that is most often found at any Kazakh meal is tea. Black tea from India and Ceylon is preferred to the cheaper loose, brick tea that comes from China. Brick tea is made from compressed tea leaves. The brick form makes it easier to transport and store. There are many qualities of brick tea; the poorest has twigs and impurities mixed with the tea leaves. The Kazakhs drink tea all the time, both as a thirst quencher and to wash down their food. Green tea is popular in the southern regions of the country where it is drunk plain without sugar or milk.

Coffee, while not as popular as tea, is also a common drink. Sweet black coffee is the norm. A stronger coffee, much like Turkish coffee, is sometimes made by bringing the coffee to a boil a few times in a small coffee pot. Each time the coffee boils, it is quickly taken off the fire and a cold metal utensil like a spoon put in it to cool down the drink. This aromatic brew is served in small cups; glasses of cold water are served on the side to wash down the coffee.

Kazakhs, whether rich or poor, are always happy to welcome guests for a feast in their homes. The women of the steppes are known for the beauty of their knit shawls.

ULTIMATE HOSPITALITY

The ultimate in Kazakh hospitality is the *dastarban*, a centuries-old tradition of receiving and serving guests. It begins with tea, often accompanied with cream, butter, jam, dried and fresh fruit, nuts, cakes, and other sweetmeats, followed by appetizers that are usually some form of horse flesh and mutton, and vegetable tidbits.

The most honored guest is presented with the boiled head of a sheep. He is then expected to carve it and distribute the meat among the other guests present, according to their importance and station in life.

Guests are often served a rich, fragrant meaty broth, called *sorpa*, in separate bowls. Sometimes, *kespe*, a noodle soup, is also served. The warm noodles are placed on a plate and a gravy of meat and vegetables poured over them.

Finally, if they still have an appetite, guests can choose from an abundant assortment of desserts. The meal is finished with more tea and *kumys*.

KAZAKH LAMB DUMPLINGS

1 teaspoon peanut oil
3/4 lb (280 g) lamb, finely minced
1 clove garlic, minced
3 tablespoons butter
1/4 cup parsley, finely chopped
2 tablespoons cilantro, finely chopped
2 tablespoons salt
3 tablespoons cold, boiled rice
1 egg, beaten
For the dough:
1 tablespoon salt
3 eggs
1 cup cold water
4 cups all-purpose flour

Dough: Combine flour and salt in a large mixing bowl. Make a deep well in the center. Add eggs and water. Mix thoroughly until the dough forms a ball. Transfer it to a lightly floured surface and flatten. Knead the dough by folding from end to end, then flattening it with the heel of your hand. Sprinkle the dough with extra flour as needed. Knead for about 15 minutes or until the dough is smooth and elastic in texture. Shape it into a ball and wrap loosely in wax paper or place in a bowl covered with a towel. Leave it to rest at room temperature for one to four hours.

Filling: Melt the butter in a large skillet. Add peanut oil and mix well over high heat. Add the lamb and garlic. Brown the meat well, making sure you break up any lumps of meat. Transfer the mixture to a bowl and add the parsley, cilantro, salt, and rice. Mix thoroughly.

Preparation: Roll the dough on a floured surface to about 1/8 inch (0.3 cm) thick. Lift and stretch it on the back of your hands until it is paper-thin. Use a glass or a cookie cutter and cut the dough into circles with a diameter of 3 inches (7.6 cm). Place a teaspoon of the filling into the center of each circle. Fold in half and press the edges of the dumpling to seal them. Lightly beat the egg. Brush the edges of the dumpling with the beaten egg. Heat the rest of the peanut oil in deep-fat fryer to 375°F (190°C). Deep fry each dumpling for 2 to 3 minutes or until they are evenly browned. Serve with rice or with soup.
(Recipe by Tamara Kostirko, Almaty. Http://soar.Berkeley.edu/recipes)

There are many superstitions about what parts of the animal may be eaten. For instance, young men are given the ears because it will make them attentive; young girls the palate to make them more diligent. Children may not eat the brain of the animal for fear that it might make them weak-willed, and young girls are never given the elbow for they may not marry.

KAZAKHSTAN

R U S S I A

Petropavlovsk

Kustanay
Rudnyy

Kokshetau

Lake Sileteniz

Uralsk (Oral)

Tobyl

Torghay Plateau
NAURZUM NATURE RESERVE

Ishim (Esil)

ASTANA (Akmola)

Aktyubinsk

Arkalyk

Lake Tengiz

Temirtau

Karagar (Qaragha

Torghay Valley

Ulutau Mts.

Emba

Chelkar

Emba

Zhezkazgan

Greater Barsuki Desert

Aral

B e t p a q d a l a D e s e

Atyrau (Gur'yev)

C a s p i a n D e p r e s s i o n

Ural

Baykonur (Leninsk)

Chu

Beyneu

Aral Sea

Syr Darya

Kyzylorda

Muyunkum Desert

C a s p i a n S e a

Karagiye Basin

Tupqaraghan Peninsula

Ustyurt Plateau

Aktau

Kyzylkum Desert

T u r a n P l a i n

Karatau Range

Dzham (Taraz)

AQSU-ZHABAGI NATURE RESERVE

Shymkent (Chimkent)

U Z B E K I S T A N

TURKMENISTAN

TAJIKIST

N

0		200		400 Miles

0	200	400	600 Kilometers

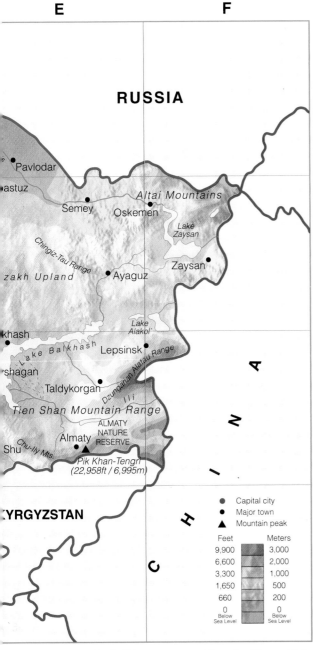

Kazakh Upland, E2
Kokshetau, D1
Kyrgyzstan, E4
Kyzylkum Desert,
 C3–C4
Kyzylorda, C3

Lake Alakol, E2
Lake Balkhash,
 E3
Lake Siletitengiz,
 D1
Lake Tengiz, D2
Lake Zaysan, F2
Lepinsk, F3

Muyunkum Desert,
 D3

Naurzum Nature
 Reserve, C2

Oskemen, F2

Pavlodar, E1
Petropavlovsk, D1
Pik Khan-Tengri,
 E3

Rudnyy, C2
Russia, A1–B1

Saryshaghan, E3
Semey, E2
Shu, E3
Shymkent, D4
Syr Darya, C3–D3

Tajikistan, D4–E4
Taldykorgan, E3
Temirtau, D2
Tien Shan Mountain
 Range, E3
Tobyl River, C2
Torghay Plateau, C2
Torghay Valley,
 C2–C3
Tupqaraghan
 Peninsula, B3–B4
Turan Plain, B4–C3
Turkmenistan, B4–C4

Ulutau Mountains,
 D2–D3
Ural River, B2
Uralsk, B2
Ustyurt Plateau, B3
Uzbekistan, C4–D4

Zaysan, F2
Zhezkazgan, D3

Dzhambul, D3
Dzungarian Alatau
 Range, E3–F3
Ekibastuz, E1–E2
Emba, B2
Emba River, B3
Ertis River, E1

Greater Barsuki Desert,
 B3–C3

Ili River, E3
Ishim River, D2

Karaganda, D2
Karagiye Basin, A3–B4

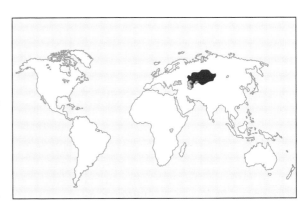

QUICK NOTES

OFFICIAL NAME
Republic of Kazakhstan

TOTAL AREA
1,048,878 sq miles (2,717,300 sq km)

POPULATION
16,733,227 (July 2000 estimate)

NATIONAL FLAG
Sky blue background with a gold sun with 32 rays above a golden eagle in the center. The hoist side of the flag has a yellow design called a "national ornamentation."

CAPITAL
Astana

HIGHEST POINT
Pik Khan-Tengri (22,958 feet/6,995 m)

CLIMATE
Continental, with cold winters and hot summers, arid and semiarid

MAJOR LAKES
Caspian Sea, Aral Sea, Lake Balkhash

MAJOR RIVERS
Ural, Emba, Chu, Syr Darya, Ili

OFFICIAL LANGUAGES
Kazakh, Russian

MAJOR RELIGIONS
Islam, Russian Orthodox

MAJOR EXPORTS
Oil, ferrous and nonferrous metals, chemicals, grain, wool, meat, coal

MAJOR IMPORTS
Machinery and machine parts, industrial materials, oil, gas, consumer goods

CURRENCY
1 tenge = 100 tiyn
US$1 = 85 tenge (1999)

GOVERNMENT TYPE
Republic

INDEPENDENCE DAY
December 16, 1991

NATIONAL HOLIDAY
Day of the Republic (October 25, 1990)

CONSTITUTION
Adopted by national referendum on August 30, 1995; first post-independece constitution adopted on January 28, 1993

IMPORTANT POLITICAL LEADERS
Nursultan Nazarbayev (1940–), president
Tokayev Kasymzhomart Kemelevich, prime minister

GLOSSARY

akyn
Kazakh folk singer or storyteller.

circumcision
Cutting off the foreskin of the male penis.

Commonwealth of Independent States (CIS)
An organization composed of former Soviet republics: Armenia, Azerbaijan, Belarus, Georgia, Kirgyzstan, Moldovia, the Russian Federation, Tajikistan, Turkmenistan, the Ukraine, and Uzbekistan.

horde
A clan or group of nomadic Central Asian people who claim hunting and grazing rights over an area.

intelligentsia
A group of educated people forming a distinct social class in society.

jyrau ("JAI-rau")
Kazakh lyric poet.

Khan
The ruler of a Central Asian tribe.

nomads
A group of people without a fixed residence. They travel from place to place in a seasonal pattern to give their animals grazing grounds.

Politburo
The main political and executive committee of the communist party

shaman
A person who is believed to have the power to cure the sick, divine the future, and act as an intermediary between the people and the spirits.

Slav
A member of an ethnic and linguistic group of people in Eastern Europe, for example, Russians, Ukrainians, and Belorussians.

steppes
Vast and grassy plains found in parts of Europe, Asia, and the United States.

Turkic
A linguistic subgroup of the Altaic family of languages, and a term to describe the people who speak these languages.

Union of Soviet Socialist Republics (USSR)
Also called the Soviet Union, the USSR was established as a result of the 1917 Russian Revolution. From 1940 to 1990, it consisted of 15 European and Asian republics. It broke up in 1991.

yurts
Dome-shaped felt tents used by nomads.

BIBLIOGRAPHY

Edwards-Jones, Imogen. *The Taming of Eagles, Exploring the New Russia*. London: Weidenfeld & Nicolson, 1993.

Glenn, E. Curtis. ed. *Kazakhstan: A Country Guide*. Washington D.C.: Library of Congress, Federal Research Division, 1996.

Kazakhstan—Then and Now. Minneapolis: Geography Department, Lerner Publications Co., 1993.

Masey, Mary Lou. *Stories of the Steppes*. New York: Van Rees Press, David McKay Co., 1968.

www.president.kz (official website maintained by the president of Kazakhstan)

INDEX

INDEX

INDEX

nature reserve, 13, 14
Nauryz, 105, 106, 107
Nazarbayev, Nursultan, 16, 30, 31, 33, 34, 36, 39, 54, 67, 78, 79, 82
newspapers, 84, 85
nomads, 15, 21, 23, 25, 27, 46, 59, 60, 61, 71, 76, 77, 83, 88, 117, 118

official language, 30
oil, 9, 41, 43, 44, 48
opposition parties, 36

paintings, 87, 93, 94
parliament, 30, 33, 35, 36, 38, 82, 84
Pavlodar, 43, 48
petroglyphs, 21
Pik Khan-Tengri, 10
political parties, 30, 36
population, 7, 15–19, 53–55, 57, 68, 74, 75
port, 44, 48
president, 16, 31, 33–39, 54, 67, 78, 79, 82, 84
prime minister, 34
Protestants, 75
public holidays, 105
public transport, 51

radios, 51, 85
railroads, 16, 18, 41, 44, 50, 51, 55
Ramadan, 73, 108, 109
regional development, 35
religion, 27, 30, 71, 72, 74, 79, 83
rivers, 11, 14, 51, 61
Roman Catholics, 75, 78
Roman Empire, 21
Roman script, 82, 83
Russia, 10, 31, 40, 41, 45, 48, 50, 54, 57, 68, 75, 83, 105
Russian (language), 15, 16, 34, 51, 68, 81, 83, 84, 95
Russians, 3, 17, 18, 24, 25, 28, 29, 30, 33, 43, 47, 49, 53, 54, 55, 57, 75, 81

Saudi Arabia, 41, 74, 78
schools, 54, 68, 69, 71, 78, 81, 95
sculpture, 87, 93
security, 38, 40, 41
Semey, 18, 95
Senate, 35, 37, 38
shamanistic beliefs, 71, 76, 77
Siberia, 44, 56
Silk Road, 22, 44, 71
singers, 18, 87, 91, 107
Slavs, 47, 54, 55, 57, 75, 82
social welfare, 66
Socialist Party, 85
soldiers, 24, 55
Soviet 40th Army, 40
Soviet republics, 27, 30, 31, 54, 56, 105
Soviet Union, 3, 7, 16, 26–31, 33, 34, 40, 41, 43–47, 50, 51, 56, 57, 67, 72, 105
Stalin, Joseph, 27, 54, 56
steppe, 9, 14, 25, 28, 46, 55, 61, 71, 83, 97, 98
Stone Age, 21
storytelling, 87–89, 101
summer, 11, 12, 59–61, 103
Supreme Court, 37
Syr Darya, 11, 51

Tajikistan, 7, 41
Tatars, 28, 55, 56, 81, 83, 93
tax, 25, 39, 57
telecommunications, 50, 51
tenge, 43, 48
Tien Shan Mountains, 8, 10, 11, 14, 24, 102
trade, 15, 18, 24, 41, 47
traditional costume, 24, 53, 87, 92
transportation, 44, 47, 50
Turkey, 40, 48, 50, 78
Turkmenistan, 7, 44
Turks, 3, 18

Uighur (language), 83, 84
Uighurs, 17, 28, 55, 81
Ukraine, the, 7, 31, 48, 50
Ukrainians, 25, 28, 53, 55, 75, 81, 84

United States, 13, 49
university, 29, 65, 68, 69
Ural Mountains, 7
Ural River, 11, 24
Ustyurt Plateau, 9
Uzbekistan, 7, 18, 41, 48, 50, 85
Uzbeks, 21, 23, 55, 81

Victory Day, 105
villages, 15, 56
Virgin Lands policy, 16, 28
Voice of Asia International Music Festival, 109

war, 21, 26, 27, 41, 56
wheat, 28, 46, 106, 116
White Horde, 23
women, 38, 47, 53, 60, 62, 64, 67, 79, 105, 116, 118, 119
workers, 15, 27, 47, 56
World War II, 15, 27, 28, 56, 105
wrestling, 99, 107
writers, 95

yurts, 15, 59, 60

PICTURE CREDITS